SPECTACLE

SPECTACLE

DISCOVERING A VIBRANT LIFE
THROUGH THE LENS OF CURIOSITY

NATALIE M. ESPARZA

NEW DEGREE PRESS

SPECTACLE

Discovering a Vibrant Life Through the Lens of Curiosity

ISBN   978-1-63676-844-1 *Paperback*

           978-1-63730-198-2 *Kindle Ebook*

           978-1-63730-288-0 *Ebook*

"...the most interesting moment of a person's life is what happens to them when all their certainties go away. Then who do you become? And then what do you look for?...that is the moment when the universe is offering up an invitation saying, 'come and find me.'"

ELIZABETH GILBERT

To my family, friends and loved ones,

Fellow semicolon tattoos and LGBTQ+,

To the curious, who ask challenging questions,

This book has been made for you.

CONTENTS

———

AUTHOR'S NOTE

One of my favorite allegories about curiosity is featured on *Psychology Today* and is called "The Pot Roast Principle."[1]

The story goes: One day after school, a young girl (let's call her Sarah) was helping her mom cook dinner. They set out each ingredient for a succulent pot roast with carrots, potatoes, and pearl onions. Her mom sliced the potatoes and carrots and asked how Sarah's day went. The knife moved in a blur as the vegetables crunched and the air was perfumed with their earthy smell. As they were speaking, Sarah noticed that her mom cut off the ends of the pot roast before she put it in the oven. She had seen her mom do this many times before but had never asked her why. Today, she was curious why that step was so important.

"Mom, why do you cut the ends of the pot roast before you put it in the oven?" Sarah asked, peering over the counter.

"I don't know why I cut the ends off, but it's what my mom always did. Why don't you ask your Grandma?" Her mother replied as she cleaned the cutting board in the sink. The water splashed as she scrubbed away.

---

1   Madora Kibbe, "The Pot Roast Principle: Ask Questions—Even When You Think You Know the Answer," *Psychology Today*, February 8, 2014.

So, the young girl called her grandmother on the phone. "Grandma, why do you cut the ends off the pot roast before you cooked it?"

"I don't know. That's just the way my mom always cooked it." Her grandmother replied. "Why don't you ask her?"

Undeterred, Sarah called her great grandmother, who lived in a nursing home, and asked her the same question.

And her great grandmother did not reply, "I cut off the ends of the pot roast because that's what my mother did." And she did not say, "Because it makes the meat juicier."

"When I was first married, we had a very small oven, and the pot roast didn't fit in the oven unless I cut the ends off."

When I first heard this story, I laughed because I felt like it applied to so much in my life. It reminded me to question the assumptions, traditions, and systems passed down for generations. There is so much we accept in our day-to-day life as normal because they have become habits. Or perhaps, we don't realize life can be different since "this is the way things have always been done."

While this story about pot roast is lighthearted, when our reality is called into question it can feel like the world is falling apart. But it is fertile ground for our growth. Curiosity demands us to risk any previously held narrative to discover what is missing.

We all come into our truth in different ways. It is usually due to systems or people we once trusted that failed us at a deep level. Then, we are forced to rebuild our lives around our innate truth.

I have never felt this more than in 2020.

The COVID-19 pandemic was the first time in my lifetime the world experienced a global pandemic. We were forced to reckon with the norms that we have lived by for so long.

Our healthcare system, economy, religions, relationships, governments, jobs, and definition of success were all called into question. Fewer Americans said they were happy in 2020 than at any point since 1972, according to a COVID Response Tracking Study by NORC at the University of Chicago.[2] Many of us are scared, lonely, and dissatisfied with the systems we've been handed.

This past year many people wanted to "return to normal," but what if we used this disruption as an opportunity for transformation? This moment is begging us to become present and examine what might not be working anymore.

Maybe the idea of exploring new ideas causes some resistance in you; this is common.

Richard Rohr in his book *Falling Upward* says, "The human ego prefers anything, just about anything, to falling, or changing, or dying. The ego is that part of you that loves the status quo—even when it's not working. It attaches to past and present and fears the future."[3] I wonder why it is so easy to cling to what we know, even if it causes us harm. Change can feel so dangerous that we'd rather uphold the status quo than do the hard work to examine our lives. But 2020 shed light on the cost of neglecting our growth.

This book is meant to encourage you to respond to uncertainty with curiosity as a tool for self-care.

I've wanted to write this book for a long time but didn't have the guts to start until now. The events of 2020 pushed me out of my comfort zone in so many ways, and I'm sure they did the same for you.

---

2   David Sterrett, Tom W. Smith and Louise Hawkley, *Historic Shift in Americans' Happiness Amid Pandemic* (Chicago: NORC, 2020), 1.

3   Richard Rohr, *Falling Upward: A Spirituality for the Two Halves of Life* (San Francisco: Jossey-Bass Inc., 2011), XXIV.

If you are struggling to find clarity in your life, coping with trauma, or feel like you're being pulled in too many directions at once, then this book is for you. Maybe you were told a successful life only fits some containers and none of them look appealing to you, but you don't know if it's possible to break out of what you know. You're nervous about what your family and friends might think or how it might feel to leave the safety of anonymity. You might feel this ache of life you could be living if you just let go of other's opinions.

This book is here to help you wield curiosity to start living the version of your life you've been dreaming about.

If you're ready to face your imposter syndrome, find your voice, and dance with your fear, this one is for you.

1

GLASSES

"What we see depends mainly on what we look for...In the same field the farmer will notice the crop, the geologists the fossils, botanists the flowers, artists the coloring, sportsmen the cover for the game. Though we may all look at the same things, it does not all follow that we should see them."

JOHN LUBBOCK, *THE BEAUTIES OF NATURE AND THE WONDERS OF THE WORLD WE LIVE IN*

Muted blobs of color turned into a brand-new world before my eyes when the optometrist slid my first pair of glasses on my face. I was dizzy with awe as my eyes didn't know where to land. As I glanced through the window of the office, my eyes danced between every branch on the acacia trees, each fluffy cloud in the sky and the colorful cars on the road. There was so much detailed beauty that I didn't know existed before this moment. My brain began to process the fact that my world was never going to be the same again—because now I could see.

Before I had words to communicate my nearsighted reality, my parents used to get frustrated when I sat close to the television as a kid. I'd sit crisscross applesauce on the carpet two feet away from the screen with my elbows planted on my knees and my hands cradling my face as I leaned in close to see the PBS kids shows. It wasn't long before one of my parents told me to move.

"Hey, why are you on the floor?" Dad asked me, patting the seat next to him on the sofa. "Why don't you join us instead?"

"I like it here!" My eyes were glued to the show.

"Move back to the couch!" Mom said. "You'll hurt your eyes!"

"Ugh, fine," I'd say. As I'd move back on the couch, Clifford the Big Red Dog would turn into a fuzzy blob of red, but I assumed everyone experienced this.

I couldn't express that it wasn't as fun on the couch because I didn't know life could be different. Why would I think otherwise?

My poor eyesight didn't just affect my enjoyment of entertainment. My parents taught my younger sister and I how to do chores from a young age. While these were useful skills to have, my poor eyesight led me to feel like their standards were impossible.

This was a theme in my younger years. I'd wipe down the kitchen counters and leave crumbs and stains. I became overly sensitive to emotions in a tone of voice because I couldn't see facial expressions. I was confused when the whiteboard at school was always white and I couldn't see the teacher's notes.

It didn't occur to my family that I needed an eye exam until my Nana noticed. When we still lived in Arizona, my younger sister and I would visit my grandparents once a month; we were eight and five. My Nana and Tata are avid nature lovers. We would soak up the sun as we hiked trails with them. My sister and I were captivated by animals and loved the exhibits of the rattlesnakes, hummingbirds, and mountain lions at the Arizona-Sonora Desert Museum.

My grandparents live on a golf course. After dinner, my Nana, sister, and I had a tradition to drive the golf cart along the greenway to see all the bunnies. My sister and I could not get enough of this, and we made games to see how many we could count at each hole as we drove along. When there wasn't a golf game on the green, we'd even get out of the golf cart and tiptoe on the grass to see how close we could get to them before they'd scurry off in every direction. My Nana tried to point out a little baby brown bunny a few feet away.

"Oh look! There's one by the ninth hole over there!" She pointed at the base of the flag. "It is so cute!"

"Where?" I strained to see. All I saw was the green grass, the sandy brown of the bunker and the faded oranges and pinks of the Arizona sunset. No baby bunny.

"Right in front of us..." she said, confused.

"I don't see it," I was exasperated by her persistence. I just wanted to move on to the next hole.

"Wait a second." My Nana put both hands on my shoulders, shifted my entire body straight at the direction of the baby bunny, and pointed to direct my line of sight. "It's right there only two or three yards away."

"I still don't see it," I insisted.

"I think we need to get your eyes checked." All three of us climbed back into the golf cart. We prepared to head home and eat our moose tracks ice cream before bedtime.

My grandparents took me to the optometrist the next day, and, as she tested different lenses on me, I realized how little I could see before. My world changed before my eyes.

When I came home with a new pair of glasses, my dad was not happy that they'd taken me to the optometrist without his permission. I was a little confused why he'd be so angry that my grandparents helped me. I revisited this event with my dad and grandma in 2020 on our weekly Zoom call. We all remembered it similarly, but my dad filled me in on what happened in his head.

"I was angry because I was ashamed; I hadn't caught the fact that my own daughter needed glasses," he said. "I felt like I was a bad parent because I didn't care for your needs."

"That makes a lot of sense, Dad," I placed my hand on my heart. "I'm honored you felt comfortable sharing that."

"I feel like if I had asked you more questions, you might have found the right words to explain what was going on and we could have caught the need for glasses sooner," he said.

"Well, the only reason I caught on was because my brother had gone through a similar situation," Nana added. "He didn't figure out he needed glasses until he was around thirteen."

In fact, it's common for parents to miss kids' vision issues. In an article in *Women's Health,* Mary Anne Murphy, OD, a VSP network eye doctor who also serves on the VSP Global Board of Directors, says that "for a lot of vision issues, there aren't any outward signs, so it can be really tricky."[4] It makes

---

4   Madeleine Burry, "This Mom Had No Idea Her Kids Were Struggling to See. Here's What She Wants Every Parent to Know," *Women's Health Magazine,* October 22, 2019._

sense that it took so long to figure it out. If neither my parents nor myself had the language to communicate the issue, how could we?

This process of self-discovery doesn't just happen with kids who need glasses. I've seen a similar phenomenon on TikTok recently. People are creating content discussing taboo subjects such as neurodivergence, abusive relationships, or the LGBTQ+ spectrum. As people found these videos, they began to finally have the words for what they were experiencing. Their curiosity led to new freedom, often a completely different way of looking at the world. Sometimes we can be so used to a certain reality we don't recognize our blind spots.

A column in the *Chicago Tribune* explores the self-revelations that everyone seems to be having during the COVID-19 lockdowns. "Now that we are largely stuck in our homes, we have the space to sit—sometimes uncomfortably—with ourselves for long stretches of time, and such openness can lead to surprising places. In the last week, a friend discovered they were trans. Another broke up with their partner of several years. And still another—a polyamorous woman married to a man—realized she was monogamous and gay. And this was just one week!"[5]

These life-altering paradigm shifts are only possible when we embrace insatiable curiosity, and luckily, I was raised to be inquisitive. Around the age of six or seven, I used to start every other sentence with the words "I have a question," until my nickname in my family became Senorita Pregunta ("Miss Question" in Spanish).

"I have a question!" I'd begin.

---

5   Anna Pulley, "Ask Anna: During COVID-19 Pandemic, 32-Year-Old Surprised That He's Now Attracted to Other Men," *Chicago Tribune,* May 25, 2020.

"Yes, Senorita Pregunta." My dad would smile. "How can we help you?"

I would ask a myriad of questions from: "Where do caterpillars go when they make a chrysalis" to "Why don't earthquakes shake the world apart?"

"That is a great question, you should go look that up!" my dad would say.

This response would frustrate me because I felt like he was being dismissive and didn't want to help. He taught me that information is at our fingertips and encouraged me to follow my examination of the world until I got an answer that satisfied me.

In school and religion, we are often taught there are right and wrong answers and a particular way to arrive at them. When I was in second grade, my grandparents offered to pay for me to go to Catholic school. Even though my family was non-denominational, my parents thought it would be a great education opportunity. But, within six months I kept getting in trouble for talking during Wednesday mass. My parents realized it was because I kept asking thoughtful questions and getting shut down by the nuns. They decided to pull me out of that school and put me in public school.

However, we still attended church as a family, and I continued asking questions during Sunday school.

"Who created God?" I asked.

"No one, he always existed."

"Why can't we see God?" I asked.

"He's invisible, like air. He's everywhere."

"Why do we go to church if God is everywhere?" I asked.

"It's important to go to church to be around other people of faith."

"But I thought God loves everyone, not just Christians."
The room fell silent.

"Well, if you read the Bible, I'm sure it will answer all your questions."

None of these answers satisfied my curiosity; I felt like the world held more nuance than that. Asking questions at church and school as a young kid is when I first learned that there are certain subjects that are considered taboo. We don't often talk about politics, religion, or mental health in public places.

Practicing vulnerability around "off-limits" subjects has helped me create space for my whole self to embrace the messy joy of life. For example, I have a group of friends who have known each other since high school. We have a group chat on Discord and have stayed in touch over the years. But our relationships deepened after college when one of us created new Discord channels dedicated to discussing topics like mental health and sexuality.

I posted: Hey, I just need to vent. *My mental health is suffering today. I just feel alone and anxious - I keep having panic attacks. I don't know who to talk to about this, but I know this channel is here.*

I didn't expect a response, since we'd never broached the topic before, but to my surprise everyone began to chime in:
I deal with the same thing! I find that walks really help me. Let me know if you ever need someone to talk to.

Yea, I'm not doing well either. My work is stressing me out, and I haven't been sleeping well.

Once one of us practiced vulnerability, the rest of us became comfortable talking about mental health, and we were able to lean on each other when we needed each other.

Avoiding discussions about money, sex, religion, or mental health doesn't make them go away. Each of these are part of the human experience and to exclude them from "normal life" is silly and, in fact, impossible. If we learned how to have conversations around difficult topics, perhaps we wouldn't view the world as so separate. Curiosity allows us to become free to be authentic.

It's time to embrace our "glasses moments" as a collective. When we ask more questions, it provides a pocket of possibility. We get a chance to release our assumptions and embrace who we want to become.

COACHING QUESTIONS

- Have you been taught that certain questions/topics are off-limits?
- Are there areas of your life that you don't give yourself permission to be curious about?
- Explore your own metaphorical "glasses moments." How did these moments make you feel?
- When was a time that you questioned "the way things have always been done"?

2

BULLIES

———

"Sticks and stones may break my bones, but words will always hurt me. Bones mend and become actually stronger in the very place they were broken and where they have been knitted up; mental wounds can grind and ooze for decades and be re-opened by the quietest whisper."

STEPHEN FRY

The cafeteria tray banged on the metal table in front of the school library as I slapped it down. My head was hot with searing anger. I began to eat my personal pizza in solitude and opened my *Harry Potter* book. My backpack hung on the back of the chair as I chewed the cardboard cafeteria food quietly. I tried to read the book, but the words wouldn't form into sentences on the page as my brain struggled to focus. I slammed the book shut, angry that my lunch was ruined, yet again. *Well, this sucks. But at least I'm alone now.*

Molten sauce and cheese burned the roof of my mouth, and my hands were covered in grease. I wiped them off on a napkin and tried to take a deep breath to calm down. *I hate middle school.* Footsteps echoed in the halls as kids from other grades moved from one class to the next. I gulped my can of Dr. Pepper as the bell rang and the halls fell silent. My hand fiddled with the back of my scalp at the base of my neck where the skin was peeling, and I winced. Not because of the pain, although the spot was tender, but because of the embarrassment I'd just endured.

A pack of guys had been mercilessly taunting me.

"Hey Snowstorm, what's with all the dandruff?" One of the boys pointed to my shoulders and laughed. I'd been anxiously picking at my eczema and flakes of skin covered my shirt. I tried to brush them off quickly and kept my eyes down at the cafeteria table. *Just ignore them, they're assholes.*

"What a nerd! Who reads during lunch, Four-Eyes?" Another one tried to take my book from my hands, and I yanked it back. I didn't want to cry in front of them; it's exactly what they wanted.

"Stop!" I muttered under my breath as I tucked the book under my arm out of reach.

"Yea Bucktooth, see a dentist why don't you!" A third boy laughed. He pushed up his top lip, so it rolled up under itself to expose his teeth, and did a rabbit impression at me. *Okay I'm done with this.* I got up and headed to the library as they continued to shout at my back.

"What? Can't take a joke?"

A part of me wished I was in the popular crowd, so I wouldn't be treated this way anymore.

Books were one of the few things I had to comfort myself from the bullying. I adventured to these far-off lands like

Hogwarts and Narnia and befriended the characters instead. They understood what it was like to be a curious outcast and didn't judge me for my eccentricity. When I read *Matilda*, it was the first time I related to someone my age; I wished for friends like her.

As an introvert, I often ate in the library and chatted with the staff to avoid the other kids altogether. I loved that our librarian's name was Ms. Honey, just like Matilda's favorite teacher.

"Hello, Ms. Honey! I'm here for some new books." I plopped the stack of books I'd read the previous week on the counter to return. She looked at me with wide eyes.

"Well...I can't believe I am saying this but there aren't any books left. You read them all." She placed my returned books behind the counter.

"Wait, what?" My heart sank. How was I going to survive school without more books?

"I suppose you could read the books in the adult section. But it would be a special privilege; I can't do this with just anyone, and I'd have to approve each book as you checked them out." Our middle school and high school shared a library so there were two different sections for each age range. I was now allowed to read the high school books.

"Okay, that sounds great!" I wondered how these books would be different. They were sectioned off to a separate part of the library, so they must be special.

She led me to the adult shelves that housed books like *The Millionaire Next Door* and *Think and Grow Rich*. I was enamored by all the knowledge set before me. I dug in hungrily and consumed every word with glee as they began to shape my view of the world.

When I was a kid, I was a free bird who ran around the backyard climbing trees and collecting bugs. I was a wild-haired, free spirit who never questioned myself. Until I turned thirteen and, suddenly, being scrappy and muddy wasn't cool anymore. Being a tomboy put me in an unattractive category.

One day I got brave enough to check out robotics club. It was something I'd been interested in for a while. When I walked into the room, to my dismay, it was all boys, including the teacher who looked over at me when I entered the room. Some of the guys in the back looked at me and snickered. *Can I be okay being the only girl here?* I glanced at all the cool gadgets and gismos and yearned to join them to learn how it all worked.

"Hey, are you lost?" the teacher asked me, as he paused his instruction.

"Is this robotics club?" Why was his first assumption that I was lost? My face grew hot with embarrassment, but I tried to remain curious.

"Yes! Do you have a note from the front office or something? Did they send you to grab another student?" he asked me, as if I couldn't possibly be there to join them.

"You know what, never mind." I was so embarrassed that I chose to turn around and leave. I clearly didn't belong there. I found an empty bathroom and slumped against a cold stall as I hugged myself. My eyes closed as my head began to spin. A scream boiled right under the surface, but I swallowed it, not wanting to cause a scene. I didn't feel like I fit in anywhere. I was lost.

If you were bullied as a child, you probably felt helpless, unsafe, insecure, and alone. That powerlessness and helplessness can carry over into adulthood. Victims of bullying often spend years trying to minimize the bullying, dismiss it, or pretend it didn't happen. According to the American Academy of Experts in Traumatic Stress, the conventional "sticks and stones" wisdom about what kind of bullying really causes lasting damage is backwards: it is emotional harm that lasts much longer than physical harm. "Bullying is an attempt to instill fear and self-loathing. Being the repetitive target of bullying damages your ability to view yourself as a desirable, capable, and effective individual."[6] Harassment from a bully teaches you that you are not safe in the world, and (when it is dished out by forces that are physically superior to yourself) that you are relatively powerless to defend yourself.

As the years progressed, I became more and more desperate to fit in and be understood. It felt like everyone else had found their "thing" and their "group" and was relatively happy, but I just couldn't hack it. Yet I could also sense there was an inherent absurdity to the school hierarchy. Why did I care so much about their opinions?

I started to fade away into the background noise. At least then I wouldn't get bullied every day; I'd rather they didn't see me at all.

By some miracle in eighth grade, I began to outgrow my awkward phase. I got my braces off, got contact lenses, grew my hair out, and dyed it red. My eczema didn't clear up, but I got better at hiding it. In elementary school I used to tower over the boys, but they began to hit their growth spurts while I remained five foot four. My body became curvy. When I started to wear makeup, it felt like the kind of transformation in *Princess Diaries*.

---

6   Mark Dombeck, "The Long Term Effects of Bullying," *American Academy of Experts in Traumatic Stress*, 2020.

Suddenly I lost my anonymity and began to get noticed by men. A lot.

Heads would turn when my mom and I would go to the grocery store. When my sister and I would walk home from school we'd get whistled and honked at. My mom's friends would joke about the "speed bumps" on my chest. My dad started to check my outfit before I walked out the door; a skirt that was okay a month ago, now fit too snug and needed to go. I didn't think of myself as a sexual object, but the rest of the world seemed to think so. I didn't always know how to handle the unwanted attention.

A hallmark of female adolescence is the realization that you are being commodified. You then are developing a sense of self within a cultural framework that values you primarily as an object. Much of your power comes from your willingness to allow others access to you.

Access that is either given freely or forcibly taken from you.

In my experience, a lot of girls become hypersexual at a young age because that behavior is rewarded by our culture and can be very validating. Young girls seek validation based on their status as a desirable object. But it is not real power. It is an illusion of power that is extended only insofar as you can meet the cultures needs as a commodity.

I wasn't comfortable in my skin. I didn't recognize myself in the mirror, and I questioned every move I made. To my surprise, girls seemed to become jealous of me, and boys wanted me. Suddenly I had sunk into the popular crowd, and I learned that it was true; pretty faces were untouchable. I didn't necessarily enjoy this, but the choice to join them was an armor from insults. My beauty became a weapon that society trained me to wield.

I denied my nerdy side and became one of the "pretty girls." I rolled my shorts up a little higher and pulled my shirt down an inch or two to accentuate my chest. Because that's what you do when you're one of them. When I sat at their lunch table, the same boys who'd bullied me weeks before fought to sit next to me. It was an alarming change, but I tried to hide my dismay and confusion.

This, of course, stirred up a different kind of trouble. Zane, one of the most popular guys in school, was a tall handsome guy with swishy blond hair and a smile that made all the girls swoon. He decided to dump Aubrey, the most popular girl in school, for me. When they broke up, Aubrey threw the Tiffany heart necklace he'd bought her at his face, and he just smirked and put it around my neck the next day. It felt like I was in a movie, and I'd finally get my chance to be the main character.

I was dumbfounded, and then smitten. I had been starved of positive attention for so long I suddenly felt like an addict. Even when I found out a few weeks later from a friend that Zane had a list of girls he wanted to get through and I just happened to be at the top of it. At first, I was furious, but it was momentary. I stayed because I thought I was supposed to feel lucky. If I had to choose between the label of "outcast" or "the most popular guy in school's girlfriend," it didn't even feel like there was a choice. The invisible rule book demanded that I stayed; I'd finally "arrived."

He sure did get through that list like it was a game; he cheated on me three times with close friends. I dated him for almost a year blinded by my desire to finally be picked instead of picked on.

I had my first sexual experience with him, in a church. That summer there was a weekly small group where we watched movies with a projector in the main worship center. It was a pitch-dark room with few adults, and we sat in the back. Before I knew it Zane's dick was out. My poor parents had taught my sister and I how to deny unwanted sexual advances, so it didn't occur to me that I should also learn how to say no to wanted ones. The bullying I had endured for years helped shape my craving for love, attention, and acceptance.

When my parents found out what I'd done, they were appalled. I tried to stay calm as I explained myself, but my mom interjected as she talked with her hands in big sweeping motions.

"Just because kids say they are doing things doesn't mean they are!" my mom said. "If they jumped off a bridge would you follow?"

Guys would grab at our bodies in the hallways. They'd pick us up and twirl us above their heads without asking us if it was okay. Girls sent nude pictures to guys at sleepovers and compared who had the biggest boobs. My whole existence had been constantly sexualized, and I tried to show them how normalized it was.

My parents just stared at me incredulously. They didn't seem to believe me.

It took years to rebuild my parents' trust. It took even longer to realize this experience that I'd been convinced was just a moment in time would stick with me for the rest of my life.

Soon that Tiffany heart necklace was around some other girl's neck. Zane continued to make his way through that list after he crossed my name off and never looked back. However, for me it was the foundational moment that informed all future romantic relationships and friendships. They became transactional.

Unfortunately, I am not alone in having this experience. Among girls in grades seven to twelve, one national study by the American Association of University Women found that 56 percent experienced sexual harassment at school.[7] That is more than half. I believe this number is probably under-reported because I never told anyone what happened to me and neither did my friends. I didn't say anything because it never even crossed my mind as an option. It was happening in the halls, and teachers never stopped it.

When girls do report unwanted sexual attention, they are often told phrases like "maybe he just likes you." These words are so familiar, and so dangerous. I've spoken with many women who have vivid memories of being told that by adult authorities when they were young, and the same phrase pops up seemingly everywhere, including children's literature and movies. The most basic boundary that defines you is your physical skin.[8] Your physical self is the first way that you learn that you are separate from others. If we are taught to ignore that boundary it teaches us that mean or aggressive behavior towards another person is an acceptable way to show affection.

It wasn't until the #MeToo movement in 2017 that I had the words to articulate what happened to me; I didn't realize it was sexual assault. I had a "glasses moment." For so long part of me had believed that I deserved what I got because I wanted the attention. I should just be happy that I was getting noticed at all; the boys just didn't know how to control

---

7   Catherine Hill and Holly Kearl, *Crossing the Line: Sexual Harassment at School* (Washington, D.C.: AAUW, 2011), 11.

8   Henry Cloud, *Boundaries: When to Say Yes, How to Say No to Take Control of Your Life* (Grand Rapids: Zondervan, 1992), 35.

themselves. So, I believed I had to let it go. Especially because any punishment they got, would also fall on me.

Ultimately, how we respond to a boy being mean or aggressive toward a girl—including any unwanted attention that makes her uncomfortable—shows her whether we respect her right to set boundaries.

My experience in middle school with bullying and first (dysfunctional) relationship informed all relationships after this. I developed an anxiety, fear, and distrust of others that led to socially isolating behavior and a belief that I wasn't allowed to express certain emotions like anger. For many years, I struggled with setting and maintaining boundaries. If we want to use curiosity as a means for healing, we must explore where our beliefs come from in order to change them.

Later in life I was introduced to the book *Rage Becomes Her: The Power of Women's Anger* by Soraya Chemaly. She said, "One of the most astounding and telling features of the Women's March and the #MeToo movement is that they both illustrate how many angry women it takes to generate public response."[9] We are taught to be quiet from a young age, and then people are surprised when we finally feel empowered to speak up.

Our boundary issues, low self-esteem, and chasing societal goals are usually rooted in our childhood. The wounds become ingrained and closely tied to our identities. Taking the time and effort to dismantle these beliefs that are no longer serving us is the only path to healing.

---

9   Soraya Chemaly, *Rage Becomes Her: The Power of Women's Anger* (New York: Atria Publishing Group, 2018), 284.

COACHING QUESTIONS

- Explore a time you abandoned yourself to fit in. How did it make you feel?
- Do you struggle with setting boundaries? Why or why not?
- What issues are you struggling with now that began in your childhood?
- How can you comfort and care for your inner child as an adult?

3

SONDER

"One can compare death to a mirror which reflects the genuine meaning of life."

SOGYAL RINPOCHE

His pale lifeless body lay in the open casket; his black hair was neatly brushed to the side, and his wrists were adorned with stacks of Sillybandz. The colorful bracelets seemed out of place in stark contrast to his gray suit and pallid skin. Reality struck the wind out of me, and I gasped for breath.

He's really gone.

My mind tried to wrap around this truth, but this was my first funeral. Death had been some distant abstract concept that happened when you were old. Before I saw his face laying there, I hoped it was a joke; he'd come back to school, and we'd all get a chance to treat him better. Two weeks ago, he was in choir class being his loud boisterous self. Now, I'd never hear his voice again or get my chance to apologize. My hand twitched at the thought and my nails sunk into my arm.

My legs were cinder blocks as I willed them to find a seat near the back of the auditorium and adjusted my black dress. *I'm a horrible person.* My hands desperately searched for something to fidget with and found my stretchy yellow bracelet. As I plucked, it snapped against my wrist repetitively. *You didn't know this would happen. How could you have possibly known?*

But that didn't really matter. After being bullied for years, I'd become the thing I hated. Now, I'd never get the chance to tell him I was sorry.

The service began, punctuated by the honks of blown noses and tearful hiccups.

While Liam's friends and family talked on stage, pictures and videos flashed from a projector. My heart sank. The more I learned about his life, I realized Liam and I could have easily been close friends. This is the first time I understood what Sonder meant—the realization that each random passerby is living a life as vivid and complex as your own.[10] We had a lot in common—a love of music and big dreams for college. Now, he'd never get a chance to see them through. The finality of it was painful. I was furious with myself for not getting to know him more and judging him so harshly.

Hot tears rolled down my cheeks as I thought back on how we met.

I was so excited to start my freshman year of high school. The linoleum halls smelled like they'd just been cleaned with Clorox as everyone walked to their first class. The choir teacher was playing a CD with guitar music that filled the hallway. My stomach was doing the salsa, and I walked

---

10   John Koenig, "Sonder," *The Dictionary of Obscure Sorrows* (blog), Oct 26, 2014, accessed January 30, 2021.

towards the choir room with anticipation. The empty room twinkled with possibility.

I loved to arrive early so I could choose a seat in the back and save a spot for my two friends. Then, I didn't have to sit by anyone unexpectedly. Or maybe it was because my mom was a self-proclaimed military brat, and I had learned that early was on-time, and on-time was late. Either way, it was a comfort to have a semblance of control when life felt chaotic. Starting ninth grade was a big transition, a fire hose of new information and social constructs. I had to make sure I didn't miss this chance to avoid the circus that middle school had been.

I stepped into the front entryway, dreaming of how awesome this year was going to be, and saw movement out of the corner of my eye. A guy with jet black feathered hair, a toothy smile, and kind brown eyes met my gaze. He'd been sitting alone in the back corner of the classroom strumming a guitar.

I guess it wasn't a CD. I weighed whether I wanted to just turn around and act like I needed to use the bathroom, to get out of the awkward social interaction.

My head jerked down to stare at the floor, and I tried to make a beeline for the back row of chairs. I was not in the mood to talk to someone new so early in the morning. A conversation like that required extra energy, and I didn't have a whole lot as I took in all the newness of high school.

Please don't talk to me.

"Hey! My name is Liam but call me Lychee. It's my favorite fruit! Who are you?" he asked warmly, standing right in front of me. It was impossible to ignore him.

"I'm Natalie!" I looked over his shoulder to indicate that I wanted to walk past him.

"Nice to meet you, Natalie! What is your favorite song?" he asked loudly. My ears rang as other student's awkwardly shimmied past us. This was becoming increasingly uncomfortable. He tilted his head to the side and looked at me curiously as he waited for me to answer.

"I love Owl City..." I wracked my brain for an actual song by the band. The desire to escape made it difficult to think.

"No way! I love their songs!" he said as he finally moved. The class had filled up, and we both took a seat next to each other. "My favorite is..."

"'Fireflies'!" we said in unison. He hummed the chorus, and I started to think maybe I'd made a new friend after all.

"I've got these cool new bracelets I collect called Sillybandz." He pulled out a bag stuffed with thin rubbery bracelets in every shape and color imaginable. Green dollar signs, blue stars, and red hearts spilled onto the floor and he bent down to pick them up. They smelled like sweaty plastic. "I have extra! The yellow phoenix is super rare, do you want one?"

"Sure, I guess." He wrapped one around my wrist. Aren't these for elementary school kids? It felt juvenile, but I went with it. Maybe this is a trend I'm not aware of yet. We spent the rest of the class getting to know each other.

He had moved here recently and was a sophomore. He wanted to make a career as a musician and be a professional guitarist. One morning he showed me he could play "Fireflies" on the guitar and we sang it as a duet.

He seemed like a sweet guy and I had fun; I was oblivious to the gap in the perceived social hierarchy. Then, I started to pick up on the fact that the other kids didn't like him.

The second week of school, my clique confronted me about it during lunch.

"Why are you friends with Lychee?" one of the girls asked. I winced. Her tone sounded as disgusted as if she'd asked why I liked to lick gum that's been sitting under a bleacher. "I've heard he's so weird, and I think he has a crush on you. You should really be careful about that," she said taking a bite of her salad.

"We bonded because we liked the same music. He seems okay." I fiddled with the yellow phoenix bracelet. My cheeks started to feel hot as embarrassment crept in. Sure, he was dorky, but we were all awkward in our own ways, right?

"I wouldn't be caught dead talking to him," she said.

After years of being tormented myself I could see the line in front of me. Was I going to cross it? I knew how shitty exclusion felt and didn't want to become a bully, but I also didn't want to lose my newfound safety. I tried to push away the thought and I continued to listen as I ate.

"I would avoid him. He's clingy," another girl said with the same note of disgust. "He's not worth your time."

I sat there quietly and thought about this conversation as we finished our lunch. Who did I want to be? This was my chance to write a new story for myself; either I stay at this table or go back to lunch in the library alone. I was afraid that if I continued to get close to him, I would get bullied again, and I'd just clawed myself out of that hole and into popularity. Those wounds were still fresh. I wanted to feel safe, and Lychee had become a social leper.

Unfortunately, being bullied greatly increases the risk that victims will become bullies themselves, a new study suggests. "Students who are victimized are more likely to exhibit aggressive behaviors towards others," said Alexandra Hua, from Cohen Children's Medical Center of New York. "This phenomenon may lead to a vicious cycle whereby bullies create bullies out of those they victimize."[11] And that is exactly what happened to me. I was too afraid of being tormented again, so I joined in as an act of self-preservation. At least, that is how I justified it at the time.

That year he became our verbal punching bag, and it felt satisfying to not be at the receiving end.

I stayed silent as people mocked his inability to understand social cues and sarcasm. I joined in on jokes about his lisp and overly positive attitude when I knew he wasn't nearby. The yellow phoenix lay forgotten in my locker.

The next year, my first day as a sophomore, he came into the choir class with bright blonde highlights in his hair. Everyone's heads turned and eyes bugged. We thought we were out of earshot.

"Oh my god." I pointed at him. "Do you see his hair?"

"What guy dyes his hair?" a friend asked. "Let alone with those bleach blonde highlights?"

"I know! What is he, a Backstreet Boy?" I snickered. "What makes him try so hard? It's pathetic."

We continued to whisper insults through the hour. As the class ended, to my horror he turned around and we locked eyes. His were full of tears and betrayal.

Oh shit. He totally heard us. I turned away from him, packed my backpack, and tried to erase the image that had suddenly seared into my mind's eye.

You know exactly what this feels like, Nat. You have to apologize.

A voice that was both my own and not my own said in my head. It would be so easy to ignore this and go on with my life, but it pulled at my heart as I zipped up my bag.

---

11   Robert Preidt, "Bullying Can Turn Victims into Bullies," *Health Day*, May 1, 2016.

By the time I chose to listen to it and turned around, he was gone. I told the voice I'd make a deal and apologize to him tomorrow. The bell just rang, and an apology today would be out of my way. I'd get there early before anyone else did so we could have some privacy.

The next day came around and I arrived in class early and vigilantly looked for him. The classroom was empty.

Where the fuck is he? I'm trying to do a nice thing here, and he doesn't even have the decency to show up.

When the bell rang to start the class and he was nowhere in sight I took a seat with my friends. Soon after we started vocal warm up exercises Mr. Harris, our principal, walked in and interrupted the lesson.

"Hey, Mrs. Turner, can I speak to you for a second?" he asked as his voice cracked a little. He did a once over of the classroom and then looked back to our teacher with a sense of urgency.

"Um...sure. We can talk in my office," she said. They walked into her office and shut the door. We could see them talk for a minute or two as Mr. Harris put a hand on her shoulder.

"I wonder what's wrong?" I whispered to the girl beside me.

"I don't know, but it's strange." She stared at the office. "Mr. Harris never interrupts a class like this unless there's an emergency. Maybe someone's parents planned to pull them out of class for some reason?"

After a few more moments of speculation in the classroom, Mr. Harris opened the door to Mrs. Turner's office and left. It took a few moments for Mrs. Turner to collect herself before she came back into the classroom. Her face was puffy and dripping with tears. We braced ourselves for whatever was next.

"Class..." she said slowly. She caught her breath sharply as tears started to stream down her face. "Liam Kelly died last night...he took his own life."

At first, we all looked at each other confused because we didn't know a kid named Liam Kelly.

"Wait...do you mean Lychee?" someone asked.

The color drained out of my face as her words punched me in the stomach. I couldn't breathe.

No.

My mind started to spin. *This isn't real, this is a joke, right? But...she wouldn't cry if this was a joke. Oh shit. Oh my god.* The walls were melting around me as I tried to process what we were just told. We all exchanged glances of alarm and dismay.

"Oh god."

Several girls in class started to cry.

He can't die. He was so young.

I started to feel my breath pick up; my knees folded up into my chest, and my arms wrapped around them. I ducked my head between my knees, tears streamed uncontrollably, and nausea racked my stomach. My body shook, and my head felt like a lightning storm of thoughts cracking down in bursts of words. *I missed my chance...I won't ever get to apologize. He's dead. This is all wrong. He died. He's not coming back.*

According to the CDC, suicide is the second leading cause of death among high school-aged youths aged fourteen-to-eighteen years after unintentional injuries.[12] The same study reports that during 2019, approximately one in five youths had seriously considered attempting suicide, one in six had made a suicide plan, one in eleven had made an

---

12   "Suicidal Ideation and Behaviors among High School Students — Youth Risk Behavior Survey, United States, 2019," CDC, accessed February 5, 2021.

attempt, and one in forty had made a suicide attempt requiring medical treatment.[13] Death had always been an abstract idea to me, but this was my first time realizing how permanent it was. Now, it was staring me in the face.

He didn't want to live anymore, and I contributed to that feeling of isolation.

It destroyed me.

For days I cried and thought it was my fault. If I'd just listened to that voice, maybe I could have prevented this. But it was done. Each time I walked into the choir room there was a void from his absence. Everyone seemed to feel it, and besides following instruction the class had grown eerily quiet. Without his loud excited voice, the room felt less colorful, like it was also mourning his absence. So many different emotions flooded through me: guilt, shame, regret, anger, denial, and sadness.

Here was yet another "glasses moment." I'd compromised my integrity just to fit in. It was a rude awakening, and I was disgusted with myself.

I continued picking at the yellow phoenix silly band as I pulled myself back to the present moment: his funeral. My body wanted to escape, but something in me knew it was important to be here. It was a small step to making amends.

To conclude the service, we sang "Fireflies" by Owl City, and I still think of him every time I hear it. It gave me chills like I could feel his presence. After the service ended, all the students who attended stood in a line to talk to his mom. It was a little surreal to see some of the other kids who had also bullied him come to pay their respect.

His funeral sobered us.

---

13   Ibid.

I didn't know what to expect and my knees began to shake as my time came and I introduced myself.

"Oh!" Lychee's mother said. "YOU are Natalie!"

"Yes." I braced myself for whatever came next.

"He could not stop talking about you." She wrapped me up in a hug. "You two were really close right?"

My body locked up and I couldn't figure out how to respond. My brain froze and time stood still. *He didn't tell her how mean I'd become?* My vision snapped back to her tear-stained face that looked at me expectantly to continue.

"Sure" I said, not able to come up with a more complete thought than that. "I'm sorry, I'm so emotional I don't know what else to say." I tried to save face. It was his funeral; I couldn't tell his mom that actually I became someone who tormented him.

"Of course, dear, I understand. Thank you so much for being his friend."

My heart ached at her response. Guilt sunk deep into my bones as I walked away from her and let the others behind me have a moment to pay condolences.

This isn't who I want to be. I was the underdog, and so was he. I don't want anyone else to die because they feel rejected by society.

If I had to search back through my life to explain where I learned the importance of compassion, authenticity, and curiosity about other people, this is it. There was an opportunity for me to be curious about a friendship, and I missed it. I had a gut feeling to apologize, and I ignored it.

I honor Liam by meeting people with curiosity instead of judgment.

COACHING QUESTIONS

- How would embracing sonder impact the relationships in your life?
- What questions can you ask in order to transform your relationships?
- Have you ever had a moment where you ignored a gut feeling? What happened?
- Have you ever changed yourself to fit in somewhere? What happened?

4

QUEER

———

"Queer people don't grow up as ourselves; we grow up playing a version of ourselves that sacrifices authenticity to minimize humiliation & prejudice. The massive task of our adult lives is to unpick which parts of ourselves are truly us & which parts we've created to protect us. It's massive, existential, and difficult. But I'm convinced that being confronted with the need for profound self-discovery so explicitly (and often early in life!) is a gift in disguise. We come out the other end wiser and truer to ourselves. Some cis/het people never get there..."

ALEXANDER LEON

"I wish I was as pretty as that singer!" Bella said, pointing at the girl on *MTV* as we bobbed our heads to the song. It was almost pointless to call this a sleepover when we stayed up until 2:00 a.m. "Her hair is so shiny, and she has a perfect nose."

"Oh my god, you are as pretty as her though," I said, dumbfounded that she couldn't see it. I played with her long blond hair. She loved when I braided it and tried different styles. It always felt so silky.

"Don't lie! I don't need you to spare my feelings." She swiveled around to shove my shoulder. The braid unraveled, and I stared into her cobalt eyes.

"Yea okay, look in the mirror some time." I blushed and glanced away. How could she not see how beautiful she was? We continued chatting until the weight of our eyelids told us it was time for bed.

After Lychee's funeral I spent the rest of my sophomore year of high school trying to navigate who I wanted to be. My understanding of the social hierarchy was shattered after I realized he and I could have easily been friends. I left my "popular" friend group and reconnected with Bella, a friend from elementary school.

When we were little, she and I would walk to the nurse's office arm in arm for her insulin shot during lunch. The first year of high school we'd drifted apart, so it was nice to have the familiarity again. We spent the rest of sophomore year hanging out, and she became my best friend. We were inseparable. I was allergic to her three fluffy cats but still loved sleeping over at her house. After years of trying to get through school alone, I finally had my first real friend.

She and I decided to learn Italian together and began writing notes back and forth in class as if it were a secret code. We loved learning new words and complaining about the boring lesson. *Ciao bella. Questa lezione non è noiosa?* We made a plan that if neither of us had a boyfriend in college we'd run away to Italy, find a small cottage in Rome or Venice and become spinsters together.

We were so excited to dress up together for the sophomore dance. I wore an eggplant dress, and she wore a sapphire one that made her eyes pop. We curled each other's hair and swept blush across each other's cheeks in her bedroom. We were glamorous. She set us up with two guys, friends of friends, who picked us up and drove us to the school. Halfway through the night, I lost sight of Bella in the crowd of sweaty teens and loud music. My heart skipped a beat and knew something was wrong. I went to our favorite hiding spot behind the bleachers and found her slumped over, mascara running down her face.

"What's wrong?" I ran over and slid down to sit beside her.

"He stood me up; he went over and started talking to his crush and left me on the dance floor." Bella wiped at her tears.

"I'm so sorry, baby girl," I said, running my hand through her hair as she leaned against my shoulder.

"I feel like an ugly idiot," she sobbed.

"You are not!" I said, shoving her lightly. "Look, who needs boys? Let's go dance together! I don't want the whole night to be ruined."

"Okay, but what about our ride home?"

"I'll call my parents; they will pick us up." I grabbed her hand and pulled her back onto the dance floor. Her face lit up as we twirled around to the next five songs. It was perfect.

But then, my parents began to talk about moving. They broke the news that we'd be driving across the country to Georgia over the summer, and I'd start my junior year there.

The week before my family left Arizona, I was packing up the last knickknacks in my room when my phone rang. I looked down and saw Bella's mom's name. *That's weird, she never calls me.* I thought about ignoring the call since I was busy, but right before it went to voicemail, I changed my mind and picked up.

"Hey Mrs. Novak, what's up?" I put her on speaker, placed the phone on my nightstand, and walked around my room taping up the last few boxes.

"Hey, Nat," she said, out of breath. "We're in the hospital. We thought it was just an issue with her diabetes, but the doctors found something else." My heart began to beat faster. *Hospital?*

"What do you mean?" I asked as I grabbed the phone and sat down on my carpet.

"I don't know how to tell you this, Nat. We can hardly believe it ourselves," she paused. "He discovered she needed a heart transplant."

I stared at my phone in silence. My brain stalled. *We are so young; how can she need a transplant?*

"Nat, are you still there?"

"She needs a what?" I asked, hoping I'd misheard her.

"They were doing some X-rays and saw a strange mark on her heart. The doctor discovered it just in time. She needs it soon," she filled me in. "We are going to be stuck at the hospital until she gets the surgery."

"Can I come and visit?"

"Please do! I know you guys are getting ready to move, but it would mean so much to her. She's really scared."

"I'll be over in a few hours."

I lay on my floor and stared blankly at the ceiling.

I was crushed that I couldn't be there with her through this painful journey. She had been my support system, and now I wouldn't get the chance to be hers when she needed me most.

The goodbye with Bella wasn't what I thought it would be. Instead of a final night of chugging sodas and avoiding sleep at her house, I was sitting next to her in a hospital room, waiting for her to say something. Anything. Instead, I just listened to a beeping monitor and her mom explain the complications behind why Bella needed a heart transplant. I had to leave the next day without hearing another word from Bella.

The movers came and packed most of the furniture into a pod. My parents and I packed Mom's van full of boxes and linens. We said goodbye to the apartment one last time and drove away.

The twenty-seven-hour trip was stretched over a weeklong drive of fighting for a spot next to the window, thanks to the unreliable air conditioning in our tomato red 2003 Ford Windstar. My mom, sister, and I drove with our dog and guinea pig for eight-hour sprints. We were as cramped as sardines in a can, and probably just as smelly, what with the pets crammed in too. Each unfamiliar hotel bed was a lumpy reminder we weren't going back home but headed towards creating a new one.

The night we arrived in Georgia the guinea pig died. My sister was devastated, and it felt like a shitty beginning to our new life. A bad omen. We found out we'd have to stay in a hotel for three weeks before the town house was ready. Homeless, friendless, and tired, I tried to keep my spirits up.

I did my best to make friends at the new school, but I didn't really fit in well.

After a few months of sitting alone at lunch and not quite mastering hallway routes or my locker combination, I got a call...

"Hey, have you heard about Bella?" Sammy said, her voice shaking.

"No, how is she doing? I haven't checked on her in a while," I said, walking home from school. I regretted drifting apart again. I knew she'd finally had a transplant though. Her mom had posted about it on social media.

"Oh god...Nat." She paused. "Bella's body rejected the transplant...she passed away a few days ago."

My entire body went ice cold.

I hung up the phone without continuing the conversation. Through a brain fog I found my way home and went inside, speechless. First Lychee, then the move...now this.

Everything clicked into place. It was like the clarity of my "glasses moment" all over again, but this time I saw how much I loved her. I had curious thoughts about women for years, but I thought it was just me wanting to be friends with them. I was always very intimidated by other girls in my grade, and I never understood why—but looking back, it was because I was attracted to them and shoved that to the side.

Oh my god...I loved her.

The realization hit me in the face, and I didn't know what to do with the glaring truth.

I saw the pattern. Rogue thoughts about wanting to kiss girls that I stuffed deep down so no one would know, not even me.

I'm never going to see her again. She can't be gone...we were going to Italy...wait...I loved her? Does that mean I'm gay? I can't be...it's wrong.

A whirlwind of emotion swam around my head as I staggered in the front door. Anger. Sadness. Immense overpowering grief. Memories that I'd suppressed flooded in of wanting to kiss her during a sleepover when I stared into her eyes and during the dance when I found her crying.

My mom came down the stairs, welcomed me home, and then saw the look of horror on my face. I couldn't explain to her exactly what was happening because I wasn't even sure myself, but the emotions overtook me, and I burst into violent tears. She led me to the couch and held me. I kicked and punched the cushions as I screamed in pain until my lungs were hoarse. This went on until I didn't have any more energy, and my mom was finally able to ask me what was wrong.

"Bella died." I couldn't read my mother's face, blurred through my tears. She hugged me tighter.

My mom knew Bella was a close friend, but not that I saw her as more. I didn't tell my parents that her death made me realize I was bisexual. I didn't have the words to explain the intense love and loss.

When you grow up in a world that doesn't really explore sexuality, it's easy to look at life through a lens of gender binary. I grew up being told that boys liked girls, and girls liked boys; that was that. That was what was considered "normal." It didn't occur to me that I might be different. And, if I was, it was wrong.

After Bella died, it left a void. My hunger for a community became an overpowering ache I could no longer ignore. After the reaction my parents had about Zane, I became too ashamed to consider telling them I might be bisexual. So, I did some research and I found a Christian youth crisis center that met at a local YMCA. It seemed like the best shot I had for fixing the thick fog of shame and loneliness I was constantly fighting through.

When I arrived thirty minutes early, I sat there in my car and debated whether to go inside.

They won't understand.

I gripped my wheel with both hands. My social anxiety screamed at me to just go home. *This place is for kids who have actual drug problems and suicidal ideation; you won't relate to these people either. Your problems aren't big enough.* I swatted the thoughts away, looked myself in the rearview mirror, and took several deep breaths to not hyperventilate. It was a crisp winter afternoon, and I couldn't tell if the shiver down my spine was from the cold or my anxiety. Each step toward that front door felt weighted with uncertainty, but I didn't know where else to go at this point and knew I needed guidance, so I trudged on.

I walked in and, feeling lost, looked for signs to point me in the right direction. When I found the cafeteria, there were three women who sat at one of the round metal tables—one with short spiky red hair, one with a large fluffy purple coat, and one with an oversized pink purse on her shoulder. Each had a sweet smile and looked over at me when I entered the room.

"Hey there! A new face! Welcome," the redhead said with a strong southern drawl as she waved me over. "How are you, and what's your name, darlin'? I'm Charlotte."

"I'm Natalie." I sat next to her at the table. "I'm not even sure I want to be here, but I don't know where else to go."

"I get that," the woman with the oversized coat said. "But we are so glad you're here. My name is Barbara!"

"I'm Avery, and I made spaghetti for everyone!" the woman with the pink purse said, as she placed a plate in front of me.

"This is an inclusive and safe place," Charlotte said to reassure me. Other kids walked in and sat down to eat with us, and the noise of several conversations filled the air. "I'm so glad you found us!"

There were about fifteen kids total, and after we all ate, we went to another room to hear a lesson. As Charlotte, Barbara, and Avery introduced themselves to the group I learned that all three of them were in recovery from drug and alcohol misuse. They preached that we were innately broken because of original sin, and Jesus could solve all my problems because he could make us whole again.

I went to this group for a few weeks, and, at first, I bought into that narrative. I saw the other kids share their struggles; many were also addicted to drugs or alcohol. As each one shared their story the leaders met them with compassion and helped them process their pain.

As someone who struggled with social anxiety, I often just listened but didn't share. About eight weeks in, I felt safe enough to speak up. When the leaders asked if anyone wanted to talk about their struggles, I raised my hand.

"Yes! Natalie, we'd love to hear from you," Charlotte said.

"I had a few friends die recently, the most recent from a failed heart transplant" I paused and looked around the silent room as all eyes were on me. "But, when I got the call, I realized I loved her. More than a friend." It felt strange to finally say it out loud.

Charlotte's face contorted from a smile to wide-eyed surprise as her eyes darted back and forth from me to the group of students. "Oh, um, why don't we talk about this after group?" she said.

"Wait, what?" Dread crashed over me. Maybe I'd misheard her.

"We'll talk about this one-on-one, Nat. As your spiritual mama, I think it would be more effective to chat together about this," Charlotte said as she interrupted my response to call on another student to share.

Spiritual what now? She wasn't my parent. The rest of the night I sat in my chair in silence, trying to untangle my mess of emotions. *Why am I always unwelcome in every space I walk into?*

After the group, Charlotte invited me to her house to chat the next day. When I arrived, she made me a cup of espresso and sat me down at her dining room table.

"Same sex attraction is just one of the many ways the devil tries to tempt us," Charlotte said.

"What do you mean?" I squirmed in my seat as beads of sweat gathered under my arms. I didn't like where this was headed.

"It's just a phase. You shouldn't pay attention to it." She dismissed the love I'd professed for my dead best friend like she was reading from a grocery list.

"So, I am just supposed to completely ignore my lived experience?" My leg began to bounce under the table as I tried to stay calm. "And trust you?"

"You'll thank me when you're older."

"The other kids get respect and compassion, and I get what?"

"We should move to the backyard to get some air," Charlotte said, walking through the screen door to the patio without another word. I was ready to leave, but I was trapped. I wanted a more satisfying ending to this conversation, so the only option was to follow.

As we stepped outside, to my surprise, Avery and Barbara were there. Before I knew why, they walked toward me in unison and laid hands on me. I was surrounded by all three of them as they began to all speak at once.

"Lord! We compel you to heal this child."

"Jesus, remove this lust from her."

"Father God, we lay hands on Natalie today to ask you to forgive her for her sins against you."

The cacophony of overlapping voices was so overwhelming I began to cry. They seemed to think it was because I was being healed. The trauma of it all caused me to disassociate in order to get some semblance of control.

They continued for half an hour and then fell silent. I said nothing as I gathered my things and left.

I had to choose between their version of recovery or my authentic self. I never went back but nevertheless, began to hate myself and pray that God would make me straight. I carried the fear that authenticity would be met with condemnation and shame for years. No one felt safe to share with anymore, so I hid it all deep within me.

My story is one of thousands of queer people navigating their sexuality in adolescence.

A common theme with my queer family is we don't feel like there is enough representation in culture. I didn't really know what it meant to be queer in high school. There were never any role models present in my life. Not in the church, my schools, or even the media. If we want to find "people like us," we have to go digging. It's impossible to overstate the power of being able to identify with a public figure, particularly when that figure is actually seen in the fullest sense.

The mythology of coming out is structurally unsound. Hollywood constructs coming out as this grand assertion of settled identity. It's easy fictional shorthand to say that when a character can declare themselves truthfully to the world they've actualized. But queer identity is a lot more complicated than that. It's not the finale of our story, but the messy beginning with clumsy experimentation with public versus private presentation.

Michael Morgan, a former professor emeritus at the University of Massachusetts at Amherst and a researcher on media effects, told the *Huffington Post*, "When you don't see people like yourself, the message is: You're invisible. The message is: You don't count. And the message is: 'There's something wrong with me.'" He continued: "Over and over and over, week after week, month after month, year after year, it sends a very clear message, not only to members of those groups, but to members of other groups, as well."[14]

Over the years as I learned about new parts of myself that weren't socially acceptable, I had to bury them away. Whether I was nerdy, tomboyish, or feeling my love for Bella, the real me wasn't allowed to come out of hiding because assimilation is the American narrative.

Curiosity became synonymous with fear because it brought so much pain. The cataclysmic collections of losses—of people, home, and sense of self—was overwhelming. I started to wonder what was true. In losing the courage to be curious and vulnerable, I lost myself.

COACHING QUESTIONS

- Have you hidden parts of yourself away for your own safety?
- What do you believe relationships are supposed to look like and where do those beliefs come from?
- How might you normalize conversations about the spectrum of sexuality?
- How has your curiosity been received by your community?

---

14 Sara Boboltz and Kimberly Yam, "Why on-Screen Representation Actually Matters," *Huffington Post*, Feb 24, 2017.

5

GRAY

———

"Although I, as a Christian, believe that God resides in absolute truth—black and white— we as people are stuck here on planet earth, contending with the gray. I myself have had a difficult time fitting into the cookie-cutter mold of a Christian. Because the older I got—the more I learned about sexuality, relationships, science, history, politics, the bible—the more I saw these gray areas. I believe that to earnestly seek God, is to honestly and fearlessly look at the gray."

BRENDA MARIE DAVIES

My fingers danced across the buttons and levers on the Black-magic switchboard as my foot tapped to the beat of the worship song. My mind soared above the church auditorium full of middle school students calculating where things needed to be several camera shots at a time. The challenge was exciting.

A giant glowing television in front of me was divided into mini screens where I could see the perspective of each camera as well as what was live on the projectors. I directed the four camera operators over our headsets as I controlled the transitions between each perfect camera shot.

"Okay, coming to camera one on the guitar. Camera two, you are on deck with drums." I switched between each one every four beats. My hands kept time with the drums reverberating through my body. "Camera three, you are blurry on the establishing shot; check your focus. Camera four, tighten up that framing on the main singer, watch your head room please."

As the worship song ended, the room filled with applause as I caught my breath. The euphoric feeling faded. My hands opened and closed as I came back to my body.

"Good job team, I'm proud of you. Take five."

Directing was the only time I felt at home in church. I was co-creating art for an audience in a sound booth away from the actual crowd. It felt like a perfect fit. I just had to ignore the words in each song as I focused on the beat instead. Any time I caught myself processing what they were singing, the sacred jargon made my stomach turn. It was a world I'd been told I didn't fit in to. So, hearing of things like Jesus' love felt disingenuous. But after Bella died, I threw myself into church believing it would save me from my grief.

Church was a way of life.

Christianity was the lens I was raised to look at the world through. My mom's parents were Southern Baptist, and my dad's parents are Catholic. But my sister and I were raised non-denominational. As far back as I can remember we went to church every Sunday. I have fond memories of going out to eat as a family after each sermon at Sonic drive through. The girls on roller skates were so cool. I didn't want to lose my faith because it was all I knew. In the South, Christianity was as ubiquitous as sweet tea and country music. Questioning my religion meant questioning how the entire world worked and my very identity. The thread of Christianity was woven into every piece of the tapestry of my life. How could I possibly walk away from the glue that was keeping my entire world together? So, I kept the quiet truth locked deep inside; I didn't want to be a Christian anymore.

In Freud's view, we create God in our own image for the purposes of eliminating the terrors of nature, mitigating the fear we feel about fate (particularly about death), and reconciling the sufferings that society unjustly imposes on us.[15] "Religion is a system of wishful illusions together with a disavowal of reality, such as we find nowhere else but in a state of blissful hallucinatory confusion."[16] This security blanket of a faith wasn't serving me anymore.

But maybe if I served as a volunteer at church every Sunday it would magically change. I just needed to pray harder or become more involved. Something would have to click eventually. Until then, it wasn't worth sharing my doubts with others.

My senior year of high school, my church had an entire sermon series warning us that college might make us lose our faith and that we couldn't let that happen. We must stay strong. Each week after the message we'd break into groups

15   Sigmund Freud, *The Future of an Illusion* (Seattle: Pacific Publishing Studio, 1927), 22.

16   Sigmund Freud, *The Future of an Illusion* (Seattle: Pacific Publishing Studio, 1927), 64.

of ten to discuss it. Our two adult leaders were handed a piece of paper with discussion questions.

"So, girls," our leader read from the piece of paper. "Have any of you ever had doubts about your faith?"

One of the girls raised her hand to speak.

"Nope! I've been a believer since I was in kindergarten; my faith is rock solid."

"Wow! That is amazing. Anyone else want to share?"

Each girl said some version of the same sentiment. They'd never had doubts. Not once. The leaders praised each one, and I stayed silent as my stomach churned. *Seriously? That has to be a load of bullshit.*

"How can you protect your faith when you go off to college?" A leader asked the next question.

"I plan on reading my bible, going to church every week, and joining a bible study," one of the girls replied. "I'll pray every day."

"Yes! I want to be prepared to debate my teachers if I have to," another girl said. "I've been watching lots of YouTube videos of pastors explaining why atheists are wrong; it's so cool to see them put in their place!"

I dug my nails into my arms to stay calm. *Do I really want a faith that is so frail it can't take my curiosity? I'm not allowed to ask a single question, let alone the thousands living rent free in my mind?*

The words were at the tip of my tongue. I wanted to understand how I could be the only one in the room who was drowning in uncertainty. But my anxiety duct taped my mouth shut. Each girl seemed to be nodding along, and I couldn't risk outing myself as the minority. No more church leaders were going to pray over me again if I could help it, so I stayed silent and observed.

"Welcome home. You belong here. Come as you are. These are the messages that meet you at Instagramable mega-churches all across the world. With services that look more like Coachella than your grandmother's prayer circle. Are the lights and the fog machines clouding the truth?...Church has never been cooler,"[17] Grace Baldrige says in her episode "The Dark Reality of Celebrity Endorsed Mega-Churches" on her YouTube Channel State Of Grace. The church I went to was a mega-church, and sometimes I felt like the high production value blinded people. Where were the deep conversations I craved?

After I graduated high school, I started attending the college sermons. The summer before college the pastor did a series about dating, love, and sex.

"The reason dating has been so difficult is that you are looking for a perfect person that doesn't exist."

I scribbled notes in my journal as he continued.

"The real trick is to become the person your future husband or wife is looking for. They probably don't want you as you are now, so focus on becoming what they want you to be."

That's a condescending way to put it...

"Once, I knew this girl who was looking for her future husband, and she met the perfect guy. He was handsome, smart, and pious. When she went home to tell her mom, she was told the cold hard truth: 'A man like that isn't looking for a girl like you.' She sank down onto the floor crying because she knew it was true."

That's harsh...but I guess you want to find a compatible partner. My brain did gymnastics trying to make the sermon make sense.

---

17   State of Grace, "The Dark Reality Of Celebrity Endorsed Mega-Churches," July 13, 2019, video, 11:45.

"So here is my suggestion to you." He pointed at his presentation. "Stop dating, take a year off, and try to become the person your perfect future spouse is looking for."

Taking time away from dating seems like good advice. It wasn't the first time I'd heard it. Ever since Zane, I'd become obsessed with boys. Maybe they were the distraction that had been hindering my faith. I just needed to hit pause and things would begin to make more sense.

"At the risk of sounding superstitious, it is common that during this year off dating, you will meet your future spouse." The crowd gasped in awe, and he held his hands out to quiet them. "Now, I can't promise anything, but it has been eerie hearing all of the testimonials. So, why not try it, what do you have to lose?"

The room erupted in applause.

I had dated a few guys since Zane, but none of the relationships had lasted long. After a while it felt like I was dating the same person with a different name. So, I decided to try this advice and take a year off dating. I couldn't wait to meet my future husband.

Along with the sermon series, we were split into groups for bible studies again. This time, instead of all girls it was co-ed.

James didn't strike me as anything other than a typical nineteen-year-old guy: brown bangs hanging in his eyes, a Christian band t-shirt, and cargo shorts. All the boys dressed and acted in a similar manner. Although I was slightly impressed when he brought his guitar out so we could all sing together.

He wasn't particularly memorable, but he sat next to me and his mannerisms kind of reminded me of Liam. He stumbled over his words a little and seemed unsure of himself.

But as we all talked, he dominated the conversation with a booming loud voice. To honor Liam's memory, I tried my best to be nice. In the middle of the evening, James leaned over and whispered to me.

"Hey, what are your favorite type of flowers?"

"I guess sunflowers; why?"

"Just curious."

He didn't speak to me the rest of the evening, and I used most of my energy to try and remember everyone's names. Crowds were always exhausting. As we were getting to know each other, everyone in the group shared why they were there. On my turn, I shared with everyone that I was going to take the year off dating.

They were all inspired by my commitment and it made me feel validated.

Maybe if I just kept acting like a Christian, I'd eventually feel like one again. As the nuns had said during my time in Catholic school, I just needed to be around other people of faith. Then it would rub off on me.

COACHING QUESTIONS

- Explore a situation where you wanted to speak up, but you didn't.
- How do you determine what is true in your life?
- Do you have questions about your beliefs that scare you?
- Did you grow up with a certain set of beliefs? How did they affect you as you grew up?

6

SUNFLOWERS

"Stop telling yourself you can fix him. He's been this way for a long, long time and he doesn't intend to change. Don't be a sacrificial lamb on the altar of his rage. Don't play the martyr to his hate. You can never save someone by letting them destroy you. That's not love, that is relational suicide. Save yourself instead. Get out while there is still time."

JOHN MARK GREEN, "OPEN LETTER TO CRYSTAL HILL PENNINGTON, A VICTIM OF DOMESTIC ABUSE"

His booming voice burrowed into my ears as my stomach churned. The vein on his flaming forehead pulsed with every word he whipped at me. My brain flooded with fear. I vaguely remembered the beginning of the fight, angry whispers flung between each other during the sermon. He wouldn't shut up when I just wanted to listen in peace. When I left to "go to the bathroom," he followed close behind me. I had always wondered why women stayed in abusive relationships. Now here I was, a freshman in college, getting screamed at by my boyfriend.

"Don't ever tell me you won't get engaged to me again." His voice echoed in the empty church hallway. He grabbed at me and sunk his nails into my arm so I couldn't walk away.

"This conversation is over." I avoided his eyes as I wrenched my arm out of his grasp. My body was in survival mode, and I needed to leave.

"Natalie, come back here," he snarled. "You're making a scene."

"No." I walked out of the church towards my car.

The ink black sky hung above me, speckled with bright stars. Fresh night air filled my lungs. Terror flowed through me; my keys were between my knuckles for safety. I glanced over my shoulder, scared he would follow.

He wasn't there.

My car beeped as I rushed in and locked the doors behind me. It wasn't a cold night, but my body was shaking from adrenaline. As I drove home, I read each sign I saw aloud, trying to keep him from my mind.

"Peachtree Road. Northpoint Parkway. Avery Court." It was no use; in crept thoughts of how this all began.

Nine months ago, I was at Chick-fil-A at 4:45 a.m. in a black polo and slacks that smelled like chicken. Smudged eyeliner and a ponytail were all I could do to look decent this early in the morning. It was functional. My manager and I were there to prepare the store for the morning shift. When we cooked the breakfast entrees in the kitchen, the stench of fry oil would cling to our clothing. I hated it.

We had just decorated the store for fall. Red and brown leaves and turkeys were hung on the walls. I started mopping the floor, whistling to myself. A few minutes before we were ready to open, I heard a knock on the front door.

"Hey, do you know that guy?" my manager Abby asked.

"No, I don't think so." I pushed the mop bucket back to the kitchen.

He continued to knock insistently until finally at 5:30 a.m., Abby opened the doors. With a Starbucks cup in each hand, he strolled up to my register.

"Hey, Sunflower." He put one of the Starbucks cups down on the counter. I glanced at the cup; my name was printed on the side. "I brought you a pumpkin spice latte."

"I'm sorry, who are you?" I stared back at him blankly, his face was only vaguely familiar.

"I'm James, we met last night. Remember?" He smiled at me.

Oh, he was one of the guys at the church bible study last night. There had been so many new faces it was hard to keep everyone straight.

"Right, I guess I do remember you. You were the one with the guitar, right?"

"Yep, that's me!" He sipped his drink and eyed me up and down. "I was wondering if I could visit you during your lunch break."

"No, I don't think so." I eyed the other customers coming in the door, noticing he wasn't there to buy anything.

"Aw, come on, I bought you a coffee."

"So?"

"Doesn't that mean I deserve some time with you?"

"If you're not going to buy something, you need to leave now. No solicitors."

He frowned at me but walked out the door. After he left, I started to serve the other customers as Abby side eyed me. When it slowed down Abby came over to me.

"Oh my gosh, I wish a guy like that went out of his way to bring me coffee when I was your age." She nudged me. "You are so lucky."

"I guess." I wiped the counter with a rag as I untangled my feelings. The whole thing made me uneasy. "I don't really know him well; you don't think it's a little weird?"

"No! He was kind of cute, wasn't he?" She filled the lemonade dispenser with a goofy smile on her face. "It was romantic!"

"Sure, in a puppy dog kind of way, but I'm not dating right now. I told him that last night when we met." I said. "It was kind of pushy."

"Well, if I were you, I wouldn't let that one get away. There are so many jerks out there, he seemed sweet." She went back in the kitchen to keep setting up for the morning rush.

I was really confused by her reaction.

On one hand, I was proud of trying to take a break from relationships to figure myself out. On the other hand, a part of me did like the attention. And the pastor said I'd probably meet my future husband. Maybe this was a sign? Her encouragement was an indicator that I should give him a chance. I'd probably misinterpreted his forwardness; I wasn't used to the attention.

For the next two weeks, he came in at the beginning of each shift and handed me a pumpkin spice latte. After that first day I didn't stop him. The last day I let him have lunch with me during my break and he brought me roses. I felt so special.

We started texting regularly. While we didn't call it dating the first few months even my parents could see a shift in me.

"Who's the guy in that picture with his arm around you?" my dad asked one day when I'd posted a Halloween picture of my church group on Facebook. Sure enough, James had his hand around my shoulder. I hadn't even noticed it at the time.

"Just some guy I've been talking to." I felt embarrassed that it was clear I was lying. But I didn't know what to call us; we weren't dating, right?

"Aren't you taking a year off dating?" my dad asked gently.

"Well, I was, but I don't know if I need it anymore. I was just waiting to finally be pursued by someone else instead of always being the one initiating the relationship."

I felt like I had to choose between being wanted by a guy or being true to myself, but his persistence had won.

The sermon sealed my certainty; he must be the one, just like the pastor said. I shrugged off the conversation with my dad and chose to enjoy the feeling of being picked after so many years of being bullied and rejected.

A month later, it was a car crash that decided my fate with James. The sound of metal on metal after I had sleepily veered into the wrong lane, made me fear for my life and see everything clearly. James was my first call. That night, we became a couple. There was no official conversation. But it became clear that he was now an important part of my life. The relationship had already progressed so far that this was the obvious way forward. In some weird way, I didn't feel like I had a choice.

After the accident, James stepped in to help in my search for a new car. He was a mechanic and wanted to look over the car to make sure there wasn't anything wrong with it. He was such a new mechanic it made me uneasy, but I decided to let him help me anyways.

We settled on a red 2001 Toyota Corolla: the symbol of our relationship. Little did I know then that the goddamn car would always be breaking down.

It wasn't long before we started seeing each other every waking hour of the day. On the outside looking in, everything was great. He was constantly doting on me with flowers and gifts. Everyone at church thought he was wonderful, a model Christian. They loved how he was always the first to lead worship with his guitar.

When Christmas rolled around, only a month after we met, he spent hundreds of dollars on gifts that I hadn't asked for. Instead of keeping Christmas small he bought me a brand-new guitar in my favorite color with mother of pearl inlay. While I thought it was pretty, he bought it because he'd been begging for us to play guitar together despite my clear disinterest.

I didn't want to seem ungrateful, but something was off. Every time I told him what I wanted he countered with what he thought I should want instead. I was a sunflower girl being surrounded by rose offerings. He kept grinding me down until what I wanted had extraordinarily little value.

Six weeks after we met, he had already started planning our wedding. Since this was the first time, I'd been so overtly desired since Zane, I thought it was romantic, but he just wanted to tie me down. His presents were trying to buy me. To change me. It started with gifts, and then the abuse began.

One night when we were in his parent's basement playing Halo, he kept pressuring me to have sex.

"No, I'm not interested." I continued playing the game, staring straight at the television. "I thought I was here to play video games."

"Please?" he whispered. His hand squeezed my thigh.

"Stop." I put the controller down. The carnal look on his face scared me. Was I really going to have to leave to get him to listen?

"Oh, come on." He kissed my neck. "I'm your boyfriend. We'll be married soon anyways, so it doesn't even matter."

It was so fast.

One moment we were there, the next I was on the floor. He'd yanked me down and jumped on top of me, and I couldn't move. His full body weight made it hard to breathe as his hands wriggled between my legs. Adrenaline flooded my body as I gasped for air. *Get out. Get out now.*

Extra strength came out of nowhere and I shoved him off me.

"Come on, why do you have to be like that?"

I grabbed my purse and ran out of the house. When I parked outside my parents' place, my forehead fell to my steering wheel, and I let out an angry scream. Red filled my vision; my rage shocked me.

What just happened?

My brain was already in the process of blocking it, and my memory was fuzzy around the edges. The next day, he acted like it never happened. I tried to bring it up, and he would change the subject over and over until I gave up.

"One of the obstacles to recognizing chronic mistreatment in relationships is that most abusive men simply don't seem like abusers. They have many good qualities, including times of kindness, warmth, and humor, especially in the early period of a relationship.

An abuser's friends may think the world of him. He may have a successful work life and have no problems with drugs or alcohol. He may simply not fit anyone's image of a cruel or intimidating person. So, when a woman feels her relationship spinning out of control, it is unlikely to occur to her that her partner is an abuser." -Lundy Bancroft[18]

Even though we never talked about his abuse, it was clear he wanted to cage me.

He started saying that I should just finish my associate degree and drop out of college to marry him sooner.

"Someone as smart as you doesn't need a Bachelor's degree, just finish your Associate and let's get married this summer," he said. "We could get a big house and a dog; it would be great."

"No...I have plans to go to university."

"But you'd be so far away, and you'll probably meet someone else and replace me. I know how this goes," he said.

My desire for a relationship blinded me to the dark path I was heading down. Now, driving home from the fight at the church, I finally started to see the writing on the wall. He already thought I was his property, saying "don't ever tell me you won't get engaged to me again." But that phrase slapped me awake. I started to see that I did have a choice, and I should plan to leave this relationship.

I'd made up so many excuses for how he was treating me.

He just cares so much about me.

Maybe I do need to learn how to compromise more.

---

18   Lundy Bancroft, *Why Does He Do That?: Inside the Minds of Angry and Controlling Men* (New York: G.P. Putnam's Sons, 2002), 8.

If I just stay a little longer, I am sure he will change.
I fell asleep trying to figure out what I was supposed to do next. The next afternoon my mom called me over to watch a movie with her. I hadn't spent much time with my parents lately, and I appreciated her invitation. Ever since James had wanted me around him all the time, my family and friends had become an afterthought.

The movie my mom invited me to watch was called *No One Would Tell*. It began with a popular guy dating a girl and it seemed innocent enough. She felt lucky to be picked by him, I could relate to that feeling. But as the movie progressed, he became physically and verbally abusive when she disagreed with him. By the end of the film, he pulled a gun on her. As the credits rolled, I sat there for a moment taking it all in and drawing the parallels.

"Oh my god...I can see James doing that...in the future, if I keep dating him," I said, brimming with fear and disgust. There was no way to escape this reality. Something deep inside me could clearly see James putting my life in danger if I ever disagreed with him in the future. I knew I absolutely needed to break up with him.

"Your dad and I have been concerned about you." My mom wrapped her arm around me. "But we assumed if we pushed, you'd run off with him and elope."

"You're right." My heart sank when I knew without a doubt, I would have done that. How had he wrapped me around his finger so tight?

"Is this how you want your life to go?" she asked me.

No.

It dawned on me that I had a choice, it was time to leave.

Abuse can come in all shapes, sizes, genders, and means. But new research carried out by *Cosmopolitan*, in partnership with Women's Aid, has revealed just how many young women don't recognize the signs of an abusive relationship.[19] The study shows 34.5 percent of online respondents said they had been in an abusive relationship, which is a staggering amount, equating to more than one third of women.[20] Of the 65.5 percent of online respondents who said they had not been in an abusive relationship, almost two thirds (63.8 percent) had experienced at least one potentially abusive behavior from their partner.[21] Our culture often portrays controlling behavior as a sign of being desired, so it's easier than we think to misconstrue abuse as love.

Trauma bonding is loyalty to a person who is destructive.[22] It occurs because of cycles of abuse followed by intermittent love or reward. This treatment creates a powerful emotional bond that is extremely hard to break.

There are seven steps to trauma bonding:[23]

1. Love Bombing: They shower you with excess love, flattery, and appreciation in order to gain your affection.
2. Trust and Dependency: They try to do everything to win your trust and make you depend on them heavily for love and validation.
3. Criticism: They gradually start criticizing you. They blame you for things and become more demanding.

19 Catriona Harvey-Jenner, "A Shocking Number of Young Women are in Abusive Relationships - but Many don't Know the Signs," *Cosmopolitan*, May 9, 2018.
20 Ibid.
21 Ibid.
22 Dimple Punjaabi, "The 7 Stages of Trauma Bonding," *The Mighty*, September 2020.
23 Ibid.

4. Gaslighting: When things go wrong, they tell you that is your fault. They make you doubt your own perceptions and manipulate you into believing their narrative.

5. Resigning to Control: You no longer know what to believe but your only way of experiencing the good feelings of Stage I is by giving in and doing things their way.

6. Loss of Self: When you fight back, things get worse. You settle for anything to have some peace and make the fights stop. You lose all your confidence.

7. Addiction: You get addicted to the highs and lows. Your body is on a constant cortisol high (stress) and craves dopamine (pleasure). This creates a cycle of dependency that feels a lot like a drug addiction.

It disgusted me that I'd consider throwing away all my family and friends just to be picked by some guy. But at the time, I didn't know what trauma bonding was. I was an addict, and it was time for me to get clean.

One of the questions that is often asked of women in abusive relationships is "Why doesn't she just leave?" I used to ask the same thing before I'd ever experienced one. But there are quite a few reasons. Isolation, shame, denial, low confidence, danger, and fear are just a few that Women's Aid UK explores.[24] Abusers often isolate their victims from family and friends, making it extremely difficult to seek support. Perpetrators are often well respected or liked in their communities because they are charming and manipulative. This prevents people from recognizing the abuse and isolates the abused further. The perpetrator often minimizes, denies,

---

24 "Why Don't Women Leave Abusive Relationships?," Womens Aid UK, accessed January 30, 2021.

or blames the abuse on the victim. Victims may be ashamed or make excuses to themselves and others to cover up the abuse. So, choosing to leave takes a lot of courage and energy.

When I chose to break up with James it was like comprising a heist; I had to come up with a location, an escape route, and multiple solutions for the manipulations he might try to pull.

I chose to break up with him at Chick-fil-A since it was a public place that I knew well. I sat down at a table with four seats, putting a large purse in the chair next to me so he couldn't sit close when he arrived. I waited nervously for his head to poke through the door. He came in with a fresh haircut and nice outfit and smiled at me. My stomach turned at the false kindness he wanted so desperately to portray to the public. He moved towards me to put his arms around me in a hug, and I just put up a hand and said, "Don't touch me."

He gave me a small, confused look. There was an air of confidence that he had complete control over the situation despite my obstinacy. As he sat down across from me, I gathered all my courage and just spit it out.

"I am breaking up with you." I saw tears begin to make his eyes shiny. Despite his confident demeanor, I was always surprised by the swiftness that he could be brought to tears. Whether it was actual devastation or mere manipulation I will never know, but with gleaming eyes, he hunched over, and his face contorted like a kicked puppy.

"Why are you doing this to me?" His lip quivered as he painted himself as the victim.

My mind buzzed.

Why did you do everything you did to me?

Why have you been so adamant about me quitting college and becoming a wife?

Why was me being independent a threat to your manhood? Why were you allowed to constantly tell me ways I could "improve" myself and therefore solidified the idea that I would never be good enough?

He kept repeating his question.

"Why are you doing this to me...why are you doing this to me?" I refused to give him any ammunition to twist my words and try to win me back. I knew if I let this become a conversation, I'd likely fold.

"I don't need to explain myself. I am done."

"Fine!" He got up from his seat so quickly that his chair fell to the floor with a loud bang. Without a second glance he stepped over it and stormed out of the building.

My body went numb, realizing I was finally free. I got up from the table, righted the chair, and went to order some food.

Standing in line I began to read the menu. A hand closed around my shoulder like a vice and pulled me off balance.

"Come outside with me and talk this over." My heart jumped. My feet slid along the floor as James tried to drag me to his car.

"No!" His nails dug into my shirt as I pulled myself free from his grasp.

Abby met my eyes. I nodded to her, signaling for her to step in, as I dashed around the counter into the kitchen.

"Sir, you need to leave."

After he'd been removed from the building, I sat there pushing the chicken around my plate as Abby tried to console me, too shaken to eat. But after dinner, just as I was pulling into my parents' neighborhood, I saw a familiar green mustang parked outside their house. A chill ran down my spine as I pulled a U-turn. Normally, I would have called my dad to come out to shoo him away, but my parents were out of town. So, I called the police at a local coffee shop. It was draining to explain to the officer the reason I was afraid for my life. It felt like he wasn't taking me seriously, like I was being dramatic. By the time the officer finally drove over to my house with me, James was gone. I thanked the officer, wondering what would happen next.

The next day there were sunflowers on the hood of my car and presumably an apology note from James. *Well look at that, you were listening. You just didn't give a shit about what I wanted.* The paper was folded in half, stuck under a windshield wiper. The thought of him being right outside as I slept made me sick to my stomach.

I didn't bother to read it. Instead, I unceremoniously threw his bullshit excuse for reconciliation in the trash, along with any last ties I may have felt to him.

I was finally free.

COACHING QUESTIONS
- Have you ever experienced an abusive relationship?
- What were the indicators that I was in an abusive relationship? What signs were there, if any?
- Have you ever made a decision based on what other people said was a good idea, ignoring your own feelings? How did that go?

7

THERAPY

———

"You can't selectively numb feelings. So, if you try to numb the vulnerability, you also numb joy, happiness, and connection."

JONATHAN VAN NESS

"Hey, Natalie! It is so good to meet you." The therapist smiled warmly as we walked down the hallway to her office. Her tight blond curls bouncing with every step. "Would you like some tea?"

"Sure, that would be great." I sat on the gray loveseat between two bright yellow pillows.

Walking into a therapist's office for the first time after leaving James felt like utter defeat. Asking for help felt like admitting a weakness. I didn't know anyone else who went to therapy, and this just gave me one more way of being an outcast.

The purple room felt funky and eclectic. A trendy lamp perched on her side table—a carved stump of wood. Paintings of the beach hung on her walls. I took a deep breath of the air perfumed with orange and frankincense and a wave of calm came over me. It was like I was in a friend's living room. I was expecting it to look like a sterile doctor's office, but this felt warm and inviting.

When she handed me the mug of chamomile and honey, I noticed her phoenix tattoo on her wrist. My shoulders relaxed as I took another deep breath. She seemed cool, not clinical.

"What brings you in today?"

"Well...my parents are making me...but also I just got out of an abusive relationship." I was not sure where to even begin as my palms began to sweat. My foot tapping on the floor, betrayed my anxiety. "I don't even know if I want to be here, but I'm willing to give it a try."

"Well, I want you to know you have full confidentiality here." She sipped her tea and picked up a legal pad. "Tell me more about the breakup."

"Letting him go has felt like getting clean from an addiction." I glanced at the beach painting on her wall, hating that a part of me missed the regularity of having him in my life. "There is this huge vacuum in my life because we used to spend every waking moment together."

I told her everything I could remember. How we met. How he quickly became controlling and wanted to be around me all the time until it felt like I couldn't breathe. The fight in the church. The dramatic break up at Chick-fil-A and calling the police. And finally, the irony of his apology bouquet that betrayed the truth. He always knew what I wanted but wasn't willing to give it to me unless it was a last-ditch effort to buy me back.

I paused to catch my breath, and she looked at me with a calm attentiveness.

"Wow, that sure is a lot." She put down her notebook and smiled at me. "Now, you've talked a lot about the breakup, and I appreciate that, but I'd like to get to know you more. What do you like?"

While it was easy to tell her about James, my mind grasped for an answer about me.

After a few moments, I came up with nothing. All that came to mind were all the ways I was a failure. Over the past few months, I hadn't done much of anything I wanted to do. I'd lost sight of what it felt like to desire anything.

Why can't I think of anything positive? It's not that hard of a question.

I hadn't given my desires much attention lately because I thought managing conflict was more important than getting what I actually wanted. This was the case with my parents, my peers, and James. I shrank so much that I had no idea what I felt or liked. My finger began tapping the side table and my breathing sped up as I slid down a panic spiral.

"I don't know." I tried to find words to explain the malfunction happening in my brain. "The fact that I can't give you a straight answer scares the shit out of me."

"Okay, well, how about we start with basics," she said. "Your homework assignment is to make a list of things you notice throughout the next two weeks that you like. It can be anything as simple as adjusting your car seat an inch to be more comfortable when you drive, to what drink you like to order at Starbucks. Anything goes, just spend time noticing."

I committed to the assignment, and it was like I was meeting myself for the first time without the filter of other people's expectations. I let go of what my parents, teachers, church leaders, and romantic interests thought I should do.

I started getting curious again.

What did I want? What did I like?

I had the epiphany that I could buy my own flowers instead of waiting for some future boyfriend to buy them for me. Putting a vase of sunflowers on my nightstand felt like an act of defiance.

This is what I like.

James had always told me to keep my hair long and not dye it. So, I cut it to my shoulders and dyed it purple.

Is this what enjoying life feels like?

I spent more time in nature. Getting present helped me realize that I missed listening to podcasts, reading books, and learning new skills. When I was dating James, I'd given up most of what I loved to make room for him, so it was freeing to make space for the things I wanted. It felt like redecorating my life. It was empowering.

Who am I and where am I going?

Ever since I broke up with James, I hadn't picked a college to transfer to once I finished my two years at community college. With all his pushing to just get an associate degree and then marry him, I'd put the choice on the back burner.

Now that I had this therapy homework, I sat down and started to do research on where I wanted to go next. During the search, I realized I'd picked a degree in computer science to mimic my dad and his career. I had been compromising all my wants in my romantic life and it turns out, I was doing it in my academic life too! I wasn't even studying a major of my own interest. So, I made a change.

Instead of trying to follow in my dad's footsteps, I knew I wanted to go into communications. Then, I stumbled upon a school that was in my budget, had a major I was interested in pursuing, and was in a small town. I figured as an introvert it would be a perfect fit. Their school colors were purple and silver, like it was meant to be.

During my second appointment my therapist suggested that I try dialectical behavior therapy to learn better emotion regulation skills. This allowed me to repair the relationship with my dad. He and I had been butting heads ever since I'd broken up with Zane all the way through ending my relationship with James. I wanted to be closer, and DBT helped give me more space in between my emotions and reactions. I was able to slow down and consider how my actions would affect others. He saw a huge shift in the way I interact with him.

In future appointments, my therapist went on to explain codependency to me. I'd never heard of it before. She told me to check out Co-Dependency Anonymous (CoDA), a twelve-step group like Alcoholics Anonymous. It was like looking in a mirror.

According to CoDA, as a codependent somewhere along the line we learned to doubt our perception, discount our feelings, and overlook our needs.[25] We looked to others to tell us what to think, feel, and behave. Other people supplied us with information about who we were and should be.[26] It became more important to be compliant or avoidant rather than to be authentic, and we adopted rigid beliefs about what "should be."[27] We believed that if we could just "get it right," things would be okay. When we "got it wrong," our sense of security and self-worth evaporated.[28]

---

25 "What is Codependence?," Co-Dependents Anonymous World, accessed January 30, 2021.

26 Ibid.

27 Ibid.

28 Ibid.

When I participated in CoDA I began to heal from my dependence on James. My goal in therapy continued to be trying to discover who I was outside of the expectations of others.

I looked back on the sermon about sex, love, and the year off dating challenge and had an epiphany. That sermon had tried to teach me to become someone for an imaginary future spouse. In therapy, I realized I am the person I was looking for all along. I didn't need to become a perfect mate; I wanted to become my authentic self for me.

My power, my worth, and direction were within me the whole time. I let go of measuring my life by if I was good enough for my imaginary future perfect partner and started living life that made me proud as an individual.

Culture has made singleness sometimes feel like a disease. And women are taught to think of themselves as preparing for a future husband. I'm so sick of that point of view, seeing articles with the titles "Four Ways to Prepare for Marriage with No Future Spouse in Sight" and "Preparing to Become an Eternal Companion." I've realized I don't know if I want to get married, and I don't want that to prevent me from living a good life. Embracing curiosity with a therapist helped me figure out what I wanted, how the world operated and what I was capable of.

More than half of people with mental illness don't seek help for their disorders because of the stigma that surrounds it.[29] Media representations of people with mental illness can influence perceptions and stigma, and they have often been negative, inaccurate, or violent representations. The stigma

---

29 Jeffrey Borenstein, "Stigma, Prejudice and Discrimination Against People with Mental Illness," *American Psychiatric Association*, August 2020.

attached to mental illness is ubiquitous. A 2016 study on stigma concluded "there is no country, society, or culture where people with mental illness have the same societal value as people without mental illness."[30] I learned how to think of myself as an individual instead of someone who was incomplete if I wasn't in a relationship. It was the permission slip I needed to start peeling back the layers of social norms I'd become wrapped up in.

My passion to help other students with their communication skills led me to quit my job at Chick-fil-A and become an English tutor. We had a few regulars who came in for help, but one of my favorites was Cayden. He was a tall lanky guy with curly brown hair and blue eyes who came in for Calculus help from a different tutor. When he was finished with his hour of help, he'd come sit at my table and chat. We became fast friends.

I also joined Student Government and became the marketing chair. A few months into that position, the faculty advisor told us all about a journalism internship opportunity in Washington, DC, over the summer. I brushed it off because it didn't seem like it was for me; I didn't know much about politics nor wanted to be a journalist.

Then two more people told me about it.

Finally, one afternoon it just popped into my head and my gut said: *you don't know what hangs in the balance if you don't do this.*

It freaked me out, but it was the same intuitive voice that told me to apologize to Liam.

I couldn't ignore it.

---

30 Erwin Goffman, *Stigma: Notes on the Management of Spoiled Identity* (New York City: Simon & Schuster, 1963), quoted in Wulf Rössler, "The Stigma...," *EMBO Reports* 17, no. 9 (2016): 1250-1253.

Getting to DC felt like an impossible and foolish goal that was outside my reach. But it was the first time I wanted something so bad that I'd move mountains to get there. It was an eight-week program where you studied economics at George Washington University, did an internship at a local business, and went to special seminars and events. One of the reasons I'd originally ignored it was because it cost ten thousand dollars. Most of the fee was for tuition and housing, and it was money I didn't have. But I applied for scholarships, worked multiple jobs, had a little help from my parents and grandparents, and had a fundraiser instead of a birthday party that year. In total, it was just enough.

I knew it was going to stretch me outside my comfort zone. I was curious to see what I could become now that James couldn't clip my wings.

COACHING QUESTIONS

- Over the next few weeks make a note of the things that bring you joy (like my therapist asked me).
- Are there aspects of your life that you've accepted not because it's what you want but what you think is expected of you?
- Do you struggle with co-dependency?
- In what ways can you make more room for joy in your life?

8

UNMASKED

"Once we feel, know, and dare to imagine
more for ourselves, we cannot unfeel, unknow,
or unimagine. There is no going back."

GLENNON DOYLE, *UNTAMED*

The rich buttery smell of microwave popcorn wafted through the seventh floor of the George Washington University dorm building. As night fell, the horns of DC rush hour traffic blared through the windows. We selected a room to make our fortress and got to work. The two twin sized mattresses were pulled to the floor. Everyone grabbed pillows from each room, throwing them on top to create a makeshift bed area big enough for all eight of us.

The Pulse Nightclub Shooting had happened a few weeks ago, and we were all shaken. Instead of being outside enjoying the beautiful fireworks display, the sounds reminded us too much of gunshots. We decided to spend the evening together inside instead.

We hung sheets in between the two dorm beds and secured them to the bedposts with hair bands. It bowed in the middle, but our little tent was complete. We all crawled in, a cuddled mountain of limbs and blankets. A laptop was placed on a desk chair that was pushed to rest at the mouth of our cave. We leaned in to watch *Midnight in Paris* as the fireworks banged and crackled in the distance. We affectionately called it our (Pillow) Fort of July.

Just a few weeks earlier, my parents dropped me off in DC for my summer internship. As my family hugged goodbye, I wondered what adventures would await me. I couldn't wait to explore all the Smithsonian Museums, Galleries, and Zoo.

When I entered the Library of Congress a wave of reverence washed over me. Stepping into that building felt like coming home to myself, the inner nerd I'd hidden away for years. The little girl who had been desperate to belong was living out the fairy tales she'd read about when she was all alone.

This was the summer that James had planned to marry me. Instead of walking down the aisle into a life that wasn't mine, I was exploring every museum in Washington, DC, that I could fit into my schedule.

I'd met my friends the first week there.

The kitchen in the George Washington University dorm was absurdly small to serve all eight floors of our dorm building. It had a single stove with four burners, an oven, a fridge, and a microwave meant to serve hundreds of students. Chicken sizzled in the pan as garlic and pepper wafted through the kitchen. I flipped it over, trying to finish cooking my meal quickly so the next person in line could use the stove. A microwave beeped as someone finished preparing their ramen.

Pots and pans clanked as I threw them in the sink to wash, and the next group of people began to cook. This program was international and I loved how diverse everyone was. My roommate was from Hong Kong but had studied at a boarding school in England. One of the girls started sharing about her internship and everything she learned at the press briefing about the Puerto Rican debt crisis. She introduced herself as Emma.

"So, they basically tried to get rid of their debt on their own terms." Emma ran a hand through her pixie cut hair. "And didn't get the consent of all the creditors."

A few of the other students around her gasped, and I leaned in intently to try to learn what I could. I didn't follow politics so most of what she said went over my head, but I tried to decipher it anyways. Sitting with others who were just as passionate about learning was intoxicating.

"Oh my gosh, you look like Rachel Maddow." A girl with tightly curled brown hair and a warm smile walked in the room and interjected. "I'm Janelle!"

"Who's Rachel Maddow?" Emma asked.

"Like a late-night TV host, she's really hot." Emma got out her phone to look it up. She squealed.

"Oh my god I do look like her! And she is so hot!" Emma said.

"Are you guys talking about the Puerto Rican debt crisis?" Janelle asked.

"Yes!" Emma took a bite of her spaghetti. "I went to capitol hill today and was at the press briefing."

"Wait," Janelle sat down at our table. "You're cute, interesting and smart; what's your name?" I was surprised how comfortable she was hitting on another girl.

"I'm Emma!"

"Did you just call her cute?" I timidly asked Janelle.

"Totally! I'm pan, I think everyone is beautiful," she replied.

"Who else here is queer?" Everyone sitting around the table except me raised their hands. I was in awe of how comfortable they were in admitting this to a group of strangers.

"I thought queer was a slur?"

"Well, we are reclaiming it as our own, it's an umbrella term for the LGBTQ+ Community. I also love the term alphabet mafia."

Everyone started sharing their orientations and identities.

"I'm pan too!"

"I'm a lesbian," Emma shared.

"I'm non-binary!"

"I'm ace!"

Everyone looked at me.

I glanced down at the table trying to process this. Bella's faced flashed in my mind's eye. Was I going to share?

"I'm pansexual, but I've never been comfortable saying it out loud." I took a drink of water, trying to stay calm. "Every time I've tried to explore it, I've been shut down. I've never had queer friends."

I paused and looked around the table. Experience had taught me that disclosing this information would get me in trouble. So, I was fighting the urge to leave the room.

Please don't be a huge mistake.

"Well, we accept you just as you are." Janelle hugged me. Her warm arms were a comfort in all this newness. "You're exactly where you are supposed to be."

Watching Jenelle and Emma easily call other girls attractive was awe-inspiring. I envied their confidence to simply speak these thoughts out loud, like they were completely normal. I'd trained myself for years to push my attraction to women down. Suppressing these feelings happened so quickly I barely noticed when it happened.

Now, it felt strange to allow them space to bubble to the surface. I worked to examine them with self-love and acceptance. I thought Emma was cute too but hadn't quite noticed until Janelle had pointed it out. Practicing this level of honesty felt like peeling off a mask that had been stuck to my psyche for years. I hadn't realized it was possible to just "be" without scrutinizing every little thought with harsh judgment and hatred.

And just like that, I came out.

Not only to them, but to myself. It would take some time to get used to it. But I was tired of hiding.

Outside of liberal bubbles coming out can still carry very real dangers such as being kicked out by your family or going through traumatic conversion therapy. It can come with increased risk of losing your job, being ostracized, and even being killed.[31] As Biz Hurst says, being queer "begins with a finite moment, of course, but coming out is an infinite expedition in the life of a homosexual."[32] I knew that this was just the beginning, but it was a step in the right direction.

As I looked around the table, I couldn't help but wonder what this feeling was. Words escaped me; it took me a second to finally name it. As someone who felt like an outcast for most of her life, this was the first time I felt like I belonged anywhere. I was exactly where I was supposed to be, and that felt strange. But a welcome kind of strange.

My time in Washington, DC, was full of discovery.

---

31 "5 Reasons Coming Out Is Still a Big Deal," Basic Butch, November 30, 2019.

32 Biz Hurst, "Why 'Coming Out' Is A Way Of Life Rather Than A Moment In Time," *Huffpost*, October 14, 2013.

In between my classes, internship, and museum tours I would hang out online with Cayden. He and I would watch movies and play computer games together. He remained one of my closest friends. I started to wonder if I had feelings for him. The only problem was, he wasn't a Christian. I'd been taught to only date people of the same faith. And yet, James and I had met in church. So, it didn't follow that Christianity meant a person was good. It felt like dating Cayden would finally be admitting to myself that I wasn't a Christian.

Also, with my new confidence in my queer identity I worried that dating him would erase that legitimacy. As a pansexual woman dating a straight man, I'd pass as straight. Did I want to go back to that after the freedom of coming out? I had no idea if he even liked me that way.

These were questions I wrestled with on my own, and I didn't feel ready to explore them with him yet.

Coming out to a group of strangers was scary, but telling my parents was another beast. After years of going to church and being convinced there was a "right" and a "wrong" way to live, I wasn't sure how they would react.

My dad and I had a weekly FaceTime call and he would ask me all about the program.

"You seem so confident," he said, smiling.

"I've been learning so much about myself lately!"

"Like what?" The question seemed easy enough. But my brain shouted: *I'm pansexual.* I tried to make up an answer but nothing else would form into a coherent thought. *You're pansexual, just tell him.* My dad stared expectantly at me in the awkward pause.

"Actually...one of the biggest things is something I'm terrified to tell you." My heart began to beat faster. *Wait, I wasn't going to tell them yet. I'm not prepared.*

"Whatever it is. Your mom and I love you for who you are, not what you do." After a few more awkward minutes of stalling and wanting to melt into the floor, I told him. "Well...I like girls." I waited a beat for his response.

"How long have you known?" His face was calm and thoughtful, not at all how I'd imagined.

"Actually, I've had crushes on girls since kindergarten. I just didn't have the words to explain what was happening, so I assumed they were just extra special best friends," I said.

"Well, thank you for sharing with me. That seems like a big deal."

"It's huge." I glanced at the sunflowers on my dorm room desk. "It explains a lot for me honestly."

"I'm proud of you, sweetie. Both for getting to this internship and being daring enough to get to know yourself better."

There was tension in the air, but not like I'd expected. It was the act of taking off a mask I'd had on for years. I'm sure the information would take some time to fully digest. But I was thankful for his patience to see me as I was, instead of attempt to correct me. I knew that not everyone was lucky enough to have that kind of experience with their family.

After months of being made to feel small with James, being bullied by peers, and traumatized by the church I started to feel empowered by my curiosity. The world suddenly felt big and full of possibility.

COACHING QUESTIONS
- Do you feel like you have a group of friends who understand you?
- Where might you look to find friends that share your interests?

- When was the first time you felt accepted by someone or a group of people?
- Do you wear a mask around people? Why or why not?

9

BROKEN

---

*"People talk about caterpillars becoming
butterflies as though they just go into a
cocoon, slap on wings, and are good to go.*

*Caterpillars have to dissolve into a disgusting
pile of goo to become butterflies.*

*So, if you're a mess wrapped in
blankets right now, keep going."*

JENNIFER WRIGHT

The cold plastic was under my foot, but before I could move
back and shift my weight off of it, I heard the snap. *You
have got to be kidding me.* The dorm room floor was littered
with clothes, trash, and school supplies. Time lost meaning
as they'd piled high since I'd moved from DC to Macon. I
blindly reached down and searched the floor until my fingers

found them. Gingerly, I grabbed both halves of my glasses from the sea of filth. As I looked down at the destroyed frames, shame flooded my body.

You're such an idiot. If you'd just cleaned your room and kept important things like glasses in a case this wouldn't have happened.

A sob escaped my lips.

This is what you get for being so lazy.

I cringed as my inner dialogue continued to kick me. I couldn't see his face but helplessly looked over at the bed in Cayden's general direction.

"What was that sound?" He sat up on the bed.

I warily held up my glasses, holding one piece in each hand. My vision was so blurry that I would have a hard time getting through the day without them. I hadn't been without glasses or contacts since I got my first pair years ago, and I was defenseless.

My fear turned to anger. It wasn't fair to be so dependent on a piece of plastic and glass that had so easily broken underfoot. If I'd just been a little more careful, it wouldn't have happened. But I hadn't had the energy to do much lately, and keeping things clean had become impossible. I just didn't have it in me.

"Oh shit." Cayden said. "Are you okay?"

"No, I'm not okay!" I yelled. "I can't see!" I sat down on the edge of the bed as my thoughts continued to race. *Why did this year have to be such shit? If it's not one thing, it's another.*

"I meant your foot. Did the glass break?" He got up from the bed and knelt before me. "Which foot did you step on it with?" I pointed to my left side, and he gently propped my leg up on his knee to inspect my foot. "Good, I don't see any blood."

"I am such an idiot! What the hell am I going to do?" Cayden sat beside me and put an arm around my shoulder. My eyes closed in defeat. "I don't have any contacts, and this was the only pair of glasses I own! I can't function without them." Tears dripped down my face. Hot drops of pain hit my hands that were still clutching the pieces and willing them to magically mend.

My world was blurry, and I was broken.

"I'm going to go drive and get some super glue." Cayden grabbed his wallet and keys and kissed my forehead. "It's a clean snap, so we should be able to find a temporary solution."

My silent frustration filled the room.

"It's going to be okay, I promise," he said. "I'll be right back."

My broken glasses were a perfect symbol for how I'd been feeling the past year. My internship in DC had given me a clear picture of genuine community—to be accepted exactly as I am. Once that summer ended so did the magic, and I was trying to grasp at something that would never be the same.

My brand-new support system of international queer friends was upended when we all moved back home across the globe. I wanted to replicate the safety I found this past summer but was forced back in the closet and the walls closed in. I couldn't breathe. Familiar loneliness and confusion crept in; I didn't understand where I fit in. I didn't know who was safe to trust.

My first month in Macon my car died. My last connection to James. It has been over a year without him, but he had still been able to kick me when I was down. When the engine gave out, leaving me hours from home, it was James mocking me. As I pushed it to the side of the road, wet from a mix of sweat and tears, I could hear James laughing at me.

"Six hundred," the large mechanic said.

An offering unfit for all I had endured with James; seems like I should have been paid much more. But the mechanic took pity on me and was going to take the piece of junk off my hands. Break it down for parts, much like James had done to me. I looked at his calloused hands, afraid meeting his eyes would lead to tears. I nodded. Six hundred it was. Goodbye, James.

Without a car in Macon, my freedom was a joke. I couldn't explore the city to get more familiar with my new surroundings.

I found it difficult to make friends and started using most of my free time to binge watch TV. I gained sixty pounds from cafeteria comfort food in the first year away from home.

One day I looked in the mirror and didn't recognize the person staring back at me. She had a scowl with dull eyes and a round body. In fact, I barely recognized anything in my life compared to the confident woman I'd become a year ago. While I didn't know it at the time, this was the beginning of my chronic depression, and it began to overwhelm me.

The darkness seeped into every crevice of my life like tar, sticky and black. I didn't have the words to really express the emotion, so I always called it "a funk." To call it depression was an admission that I was mentally ill, and that couldn't be the case. My straight A's and excellent internship in the President's Office said otherwise. There's no way a depressed person could look so successful. It didn't correlate. But, during that first year this heavy fog fell over my brain. Everything took so much energy.

Making a cup of coffee used to take three steps: grab a cup, fill the coffee grounds, and hit brew.

Now, everything took twenty or more steps: Sit up in bed, step out of bed, walk to the kitchen, find a clean mug, grab it out of the cupboard and place it on the counter, find the coffee, find the coffee filters, find a tablespoon measure, scoop coffee into the coffee filter, place the coffee filter into the machine, make sure there is water in the machine, press brew, open the fridge, grab the creamer, smell it to make sure it wasn't expired, listen for the coffee to be done brewing, pour the creamer in the coffee, stir, put the creamer back, put the coffee tin back, and dump out the old coffee filter.

Exhausting.

This is how every task felt. Thousands of steps.

There were multiple things that triggered my depressive episode, but one of the most memorable was that I delved further into questioning my religion. There was only one honors class available to me, and it was analyzing *Star Wars* through Jungian psychology and Joseph Campbell's *Hero with a Thousand Faces*. During the same semester, I was taking a world religions class. The combination of these two classes provided a framework to start examining my experience with religion. I finally gave myself permission to start asking all the questions I'd been told to avoid. *What part did I want it to play in my future?*

Dr. James Fowler talks about this exploration in his book *Stages of Faith: The Psychology of Development and the Quest for Meaning*. Fowler said that what I perceived as a spiritual crisis fit the criteria for what he describes as the transition from Stage 3 to Stage 4 faith.[33] Fowler characterizes this transition as the time when a spiritual sojourner exchanges a tacitly held and community-promulgated belief system for a new system that is discerned and chosen via the person's

33   James Fowler, *Stages of Faith: The Psychology of Development and the Quest for Meaning* (New York: HarperCollins, 1978), 177.

reinvigorated sense of autonomy and self. In other words, the person moves from relying on their community to tell them what to believe and how to make sense of the world to deciding for themselves what kind of person they want to be. But that transition was painful and fed my depression. The uncertainty made me call into question my entire life. *The Hero with a Thousand Faces* by Joseph Campbell outlines the circular Hero's Journey. This is the common template of stories that involve a hero who goes on an adventure, is victorious in a decisive crisis, and comes home changed or transformed.[34] It seemed to me like religions were just a psycho-spiritual drama where the main character was the physical representation of a deity. From Jesus to Buddha, they were all acting out the hero's journey.

I was tired of idolizing these men.

Where was the divine feminine in all this?

I didn't see myself represented in these faiths.

One of the biggest things that helped me process this was reading *Love Wins* by Rob Bell. He put words to thoughts I had when reading the bible front to back, over and over. Searching for answers.

In his book, Rob says this:

> *"Jesus is bigger than any one religion. He didn't come to start a new religion, and he continually disrupted whatever conventions or systems or establishments that existed in his day. He will always transcend whatever cages and labels are created to contain and name him, especially the one called 'Christianity.'"* [35]

---

34 Joseph Campbell, *Hero With a Thousand Faces* (Novato: Pantheon Books: 1949), 16.

35 Rob Bell, *Love Wins: A Book About Heaven, Hell, and the Fate of Every Person Who Ever Lived* (New York: HarperCollins, 2011), 144.

So, I started to consider letting religion go, and I stopped calling myself a Christian because the label didn't fit me anymore. But I desperately wanted to make friends. I wanted religion to work for me, because I didn't know how life was supposed to function without it. Even though I'd had a few bad experiences with church, I'd been taught this was the way to find community. I did some research and found a modern non-denominational church in the area, a sister church to the one I'd volunteered at in the past.

I joined another group that met at the church on Sunday nights and began to volunteer on their tech team running the lights for the worship performances. At the same time, I was an imposter. Did I even belong here if I wasn't a Christian? I just kept showing up because I wanted to be proven wrong.

One day I got it in my head that maybe singing on stage would help me regain my faith, since nothing else seemed to be working. Music connected me to something higher than myself. A sense of expansive bliss and oneness with the universe. There was a lengthy application that asked a lot about my journey as a Christian, and it was the first time I'd answered something like this honestly. I wasn't sure where I stood with my religion, but I was here to learn. A week later the pastor invited me to get coffee with him to discuss it.

The cafe doubled as a local art show that was always displaying the latest pieces for sale. I arrived early to marvel at the latest one that was ten feet wide and six feet tall, a painting of a forest in vibrant blues and pinks. The painting was a fleeting breath of fresh air in my gloomy state of mind. It looked like happiness, something that was increasingly illusive lately. My trance was broken by the arrival of the pastor.

We sipped our coffee at a corner table as he began to interview me.

"So, tell me about your walk with Christ." He pulled a legal pad and pen out of his messenger bag. I cringed, remembering the women laying their hands on me to pray the gay away. Then, the high school sermon about questioning beliefs swirled around my mind. How honest did he want me to be? "Well, I have had a few bad experiences. But haven't let it prevent me from trying to explore my faith," I said. "Ever since reading *Love Wins* and *Velvet Elvis* by Rob Bell, I don't like using the word Christian." I saw a frown begin to form on his face.

"Can you elaborate?" he asked, taking a few more notes.

"I think wisdom can come from all walks of life, and I don't like the 'us versus them' mentality of creating an 'in group.'"

"If you can't unequivocally call yourself a Christian, we can't have you on stage." He put his pen down and checked his watch as if I were wasting his time. "If you don't believe what you're singing then we can't lead our congregation astray and just let anyone up there."

"I guess I'm confused. I've read the bible multiple times and think Jesus is an amazing teacher, but I think he didn't come here to start a religion, therefore I'm not a Christian." My heart raced as I tried to put words to what I'd been learning about myself. Speaking my truth to the authority figure in front of me took all the courage and energy I had. "But I want to serve through singing."

"I think you're a wonderful person, Natalie, but for the integrity of the church I can't say yes. I'm sorry." He used a measured tone as if he didn't want to upset me, but the conversation was over. I was incredibly frustrated. I understood where he was coming from, but I still felt like a misfit. Here I was again; my authentic self wasn't enough for the church.

He didn't seem interested in discussing nuance with me. It was black or white, either I called myself a Christian or I wasn't accepted. It was a slap in the face because I'd been allowed to volunteer on their tech team but wasn't allowed to be the face of the church. The mixed messages felt hypocritical. So, they could use my talents, but only in the back where no one could see me.

I was supposed to get nurtured from church, instead I was exhausted. Time and time again I heard church leaders say that if you were struggling with faith to just stick with it, but it was a thousand paper cuts. If this was what religion was, I didn't want any part of it.

I can't remember a time I didn't know about God or believe in a higher power, which means there was never a conscious decision on my part, never an option or opportunity to explore other religions or beliefs. Only Jesus from the very beginning, until I got to college.

After I walked away from my faith, I was bitter because I'd been robbed of the opportunity to choose for myself what I believed. What remained was a vacuum.

My sense of identity began to unravel. In middle school I was taught that beauty was power; my extra weight stripped me of that power. I'd been taught a set of rules by the church that I no longer believed in. I had come out over the summer, yet, now in conservative Macon, I was more closeted than ever. I was so far back there; I'd got lost under the clothes of a life designed for someone else. I couldn't breathe.

Why wasn't I ever good enough? Without beauty, confidence, and community I became worthless and fragile. I grabbed some ice cream on the way home from the cafe and wrapped a blanket around me.

You should go to therapy; you can't handle this on your own.
I pushed the thought away as I opened the tub of Ben and Jerry's to drown out my disgust. With each bite I tried to convince myself I was fine and could handle it on my own. *This is rock bottom; you need to make an appointment before you do something stupid.*
I looked down at the empty tub and realized this was me: empty. I got my computer out and made an appointment to see the school counselor the next day.

I told her that I had resigned myself to being miserable here and was just going to white knuckle it through the two years until graduation.

"I'm a piece of shit." My fingers anxiously picked at my scalp. Lightening cracked outside, I glanced out the third story window at the dark storm clouds. "I fucked up, and now I am paying the price."

"Well, that is strong language." Her pen scratched across her notebook. "So, you are just going to choose to be miserable for two years? That sure is a long time."

"It's not like I want to be miserable." *Did she really think this was a choice?* "But I have tried so many things, and people just suck."

While it was cathartic to have someone to vent to, I didn't feel like I made much progress with the school therapist. She just helped me stay afloat as I navigated the rapids of college and depression.

I was tired of trying to fit in repeatedly. The world was mocking me. University was middle school all over again. I didn't know where I belonged or who I wanted to be.

I've learned that it's common for twenty- and thirty-somethings to have a "quarter-life" crisis. When I was in the middle of it, I thought I was weak or being dramatic. My problems were "first world problems," so they didn't matter.

According to an article in the *Harvard Business Review*, the "quarter-life" crisis experienced by many twenty- and thirty-somethings typically involves four stages:[36]

1. Being locked into a commitment (relationship, job, housing, etc.)
2. Ending that commitment, and now feeling isolated
3. Internal reflection, followed by exploring new interests
4. Emerging from the crisis much happier and with a greater sense of purpose

One of the few things that helped during this period of my life was Cayden. He was one of my only consistent friends at the time. As I continued to process my ex James I shared with Cayden the manipulation and abuse I'd experienced.

We'd only been friends for a few months, but he became my confidant. Among the turbulent seas of college, we constructed our own lifeboat together. My love for him surprised me, but I wasn't sure if I wanted to risk our friendship to explore more. Even though it had been over a year since breaking up with James, I didn't trust myself to recognize the signs of abuse.

But Cayden never pushed, and he was this gentle steady presence in my life. I loved how comfortable I was being my nerdy queer self around him; there was no need to hide it. I wasn't sure that a long-distance relationship was something I was interested in pursuing.

---

36 Ran Zilca, "Why Your Late Twenties Is the Worst Time of Your Life," *Harvard Business Review*, March 7, 2016.

However, after my car broke down, Cayden offered to help me find my next one. The deja vu made me hesitant to let him into the process. I'd already let one guy help me find a car, and that led to the abusive relationship. Why would this be any different?

But after two months of searching on my own and finding nothing in Macon, he started to look in Marietta. He found a car that was within my budget and had it checked over by three different mechanics because I was so paranoid. It was such a stark contrast to James. Both this car and this guy seemed too good to be true. I bought the car, and a week later I finally told Cayden I liked him more than a friend. He had felt similarly but wanted me to make the first move due to my past.

Now, we'd been together for over a year. He was my best friend. I stared down at my hands, my eyes trying to focus on the broken glasses. Cayden came back with some Gorilla Glue and asked me to give him the glasses. As the glue dried, I was thankful to have a partner who could help me pick up the pieces when I wasn't myself.

"As a culture, we all think that age twenty-five is the best stage of our life—these folks are happy, they're doing everything they want and it's a great time of life," American Counseling Association (ACA) member Cyrus Williams said. "We really need to acknowledge and not minimize this time period."[37]

I wish I could have been more prepared to meet this time of my life with curiosity.

Why was I so tired?

---

37 Lynne Shallcross, "Validating the Quarter-Life Crisis," *Counseling Today,* April 22, 2016.

Why did I need to find community in church?

Why was I hiding myself?

If I'd learned to ask the right questions, and not be afraid of doubts or changing my opinions, I might have found the help I needed sooner. But I didn't get the right help for my depression until after graduation. I thought it was situational; Macon was the issue. I didn't consider that maybe the problems I was experiencing were much deeper rooted than that.

COACHING QUESTIONS

- Have you ever been stuck in a period you labeled just a funk? Explore that time.
- In times of isolation, who have you been able to turn to? Who has served as your constant?
- Are you able to fully express who you are in your community?

10

DISSENT

———

"We can choose courage, or we can choose comfort, but we can't have both. Not at the same time."

BRENÉ BROWN, *RISING STRONG*

The noxious fumes flooded my dorm room, like rotten eggs. I grabbed for my phone, glancing down at the glowing screen. *Two in the morning!* Before my mind could piece together what was happening, there was pounding on my front door. I went outside and sewer fumes and tired students filled the breezeway. As the Resident Assistant for the building, it was on my shoulders to fix this. I dreaded calling Tamira, the Resident Assistant Coordinator, who didn't seem to like me at all, but I was in over my head.

"Hey, I'm sorry it's such a crappy time of day but our building is filling with sewer water. I need help."

"Okay, I'll call a plumber. Tell everyone to just go back to bed." Her son started to cry in the background. She huffed. The line clicked before I could say anything else.

This is crazy, why isn't she treating this urgently? There is no way we are going to be able to sleep in this stench.

I started texting my parents in a panic: *My building is filled with sewage water, and besides calling a plumber, my bosses are dismissing how serious this is.*

My mom, a nurse, replied: *That is a biohazard. You are the person in charge here—you must get the students out of that building.*

Pacing my room, my fingers flew across the screen: *What am I supposed to do? I'm on probation and don't want to lose my housing.*

My mom replied: *What is more important? If you are doing your job, they shouldn't be able to fire you. If they do, we will figure it out.*

I knew she was right, but I was seconds away from flopping on my bed to get a few precious hours of sleep. I was tired of constantly fighting my administrators, just for doing my job. Holding myself together was hard enough let alone caring for a building of forty-eight other students.

A few months ago, soon after I became an RA, we were told there would be construction in between semesters. It was annoying, but I tried to get out of the dorm a lot to avoid the noise.

One day I came home, and my foot caught on something in the breezeway. At the bottom floor of the dorm building, I counted five different types of saws, plugged in and blades uncovered. I got my phone out, snapped some photos and headed for Tamira's office.

"Hey, have you seen my building's breezeway today?" My hands shook as I tried to show her my pictures. "There's construction stuff everywhere. It's extremely dangerous and irresponsible."

"Well, the school hired them." She waved my phone away.

"What does that mean?"

"There's nothing I can do about it."

"So, there's safety hazards all over the bottom of my building and there's nothing we can do about it?" I was sure if she just looked at the photos she'd understand where I was coming from.

"I already answered your question, Natalie."

My hands dropped to my side in defeat. I stared at her a few more moments wishing she'd say anything else, but she ignored me. On my way back to my room I questioned if I was taking this personally. Maybe it wasn't as big a deal as I was making it out to be.

All the other RAs say you take your job too seriously.

I hated how much they made me question my own judgment. After the bullying and religious trauma, I'd had a tenuous relationship to authority figures. *Was I just being obstinate?* But something in me pushed back.

If another resident tripped over any of that and busted their head open it would be a lawsuit for the school.

Tears streamed down my face as my brain continued to fight both sides of the argument. My depression laughed at my feeble attempt to make sense of it all. I didn't understand why this didn't matter to her.

The next day, I got an email saying that I was being put on probation. When I pressed, I was told it was for "questioning authority." If I stepped out of line again, I'd be fired.

Confusion didn't even begin to explain my state of mind.

The housing stipend was a necessity to pay for school. My job was to take care of my students, but my basic need for shelter was in jeopardy for doing just that. The next few months I walked on eggshells; I didn't know what would be considered "questioning authority."

The night of the sewer pipe leak was the last straw. I met with the director of student housing the next day and told him everything. I'd been gaslit for months, and I needed him to know how the students were being treated. The stress of the mental juggling act had a profound effect on my depression. I let my building know that I was leaving. After I moved, the wave of relief made me wish I'd quit sooner.

My depression was still walking beside me every day, but I looked for ways to break out of the walls it had constructed. I looked on my school website at a list of clubs and found one called the Gay-Straight Alliance (GSA).

At the time, I'd never heard of it before and decided to try a meeting. I was nervous because besides DC, I'd never practiced being "out." Within a few meetings I was included in a way I hadn't been for months. Instead of trying to find community in the church that repeatedly rejected me, I was now going to the state capitol with the GSA and lobbying for LGBTQ+ rights. I could be there and bring my whole self without shame. Becoming an active part of that community gave me purpose to get through the rest of my college experience.

I started listening to myself again, like I'd been taught by my first therapist. In my religions class, I'd heard of something called reiki and became intrigued. Reiki is a very specific form of energy healing, in which hands are placed just off the body or lightly touching the body, as in "laying on of hands."[38] Growing up, I had an affinity for using words like

---

38 "Integrative Medicine & Digestive Center: Reiki," John Hopkins Medicine, accessed February 17, 2021.

"energy" when describing people and situations. But church had taught me that things like tarot cards, pagan practices, and reiki were evil. In my curiosity, I booked a session to try it, which resulted in an intense internal battle. I didn't believe in Christianity, but the roots of fear ran deep.

As I walked into her house, she led me to her office. Her desk was adorned with crystals, candles, cards, and essential oil bottles. In one corner there was a rectangular bed, like a message table, with a purple pillow and tasseled blanket. The air was perfumed with calming vetiver and frankincense.

"What brings you here today?" She smiled warmly.

"A feeling. It's hard to put into words, but I was drawn to your website." I glanced around the room, starting to feel excited. Something about all of this felt like coming home. "I also grew up in a religious house and I'm in a period of deconstruction, so there's some weird shame even being here."

"You'd be surprised that is what most women say on their first visit here." I wasn't expecting that response. "I myself grew up Christian and experienced religious trauma. I've found reiki to be a key part of my healing journey."

As she went through the session, each part of my body released. My mind cleared.

After this experience, I had more confidence exploring pagan and Wiccan traditions. They held a reverence for the sacred feminine that I'd been searching for with the triple goddess: mother, maiden and crone. For years I'd wanted a spiritual practice that I saw myself reflected in. The moon phases and pagan holidays were things that predated Christianity and just made more sense to me. Connecting to the cycles of nature brought me home to myself.

While the sewer incident was the first time I stood up to authority during my depression, the GSA and reiki were formative experiences during my journey standing up to religious trauma and forging a new path. Slowly, I began to claw my way out of the pit of depression. The rest of the year was a marathon. I didn't go back to therapy, and I just wanted to move out of Macon and get a fresh start. The days flew by, and I was barely connected to my body. I just knew I had to get out of there so I could find myself again. Graduation couldn't come fast enough.

Janelle and Cayden came to my graduation ceremony. My mom and I decorated my cap with purple gems and flowers. In the middle I wrote: *Nevertheless, she persisted*. It had been my mantra throughout my time in Macon.

After the ceremony, Janelle swept me up in a warm hug and held me for a few seconds to help me calm down.

"Babe, you did it," she whispered in my ear. "I am so proud of you." Her arms fell to her sides, and I attempted a smile.

"I appreciate it, I'm just so tired," I said. "I'm ready to move on."

"Let this be a reminder, to never settle again." She shifted to a more serious tone. "You fought like hell these past two years. But you deserve better. So, don't settle."

The words hit me more than I expected. A few days before graduation I realized that if I wanted to go to another school, I could have. But I'd convinced myself that I didn't have the money, so it wasn't possible. It dawned on me how much of my life since DC was me feeling like a victim who was trapped here, like I had no choice in the matter.

I carry her words with me. In every new situation. I don't let myself believe I don't have a choice.

COACHING QUESTIONS

- Have you ever experienced a situation where you had to choose between what was right and what was easy?
- What signs help you navigate away from one priority (like fiscal responsibility) to focus on another one (like mental wellness or self-fulfillment), even if they're in opposition?
- What have you settled for in your past? What will you no longer settle for?
- When have you felt stuck? How did you get unstuck?
- Do you find people in your life (work/school/family) tell you to not "rock the boat" or "just go with the flow" because it would be inconvenient otherwise?

11

SQUARE ONE

---

*"You must give up the life you planned in order
to have the life that is waiting for you."*

JOSEPH CAMPBELL

I shivered, yanking a third blanket on top of me as I turned
to my side, attempting to get comfortable. The bar of the
twin-sized pullout couch dug into my back through the thin
mattress. It was hard to sleep on this constant reminder of
how cramped I was in this stage of life. I'd moved back in
with my parents after graduation a month ago. So many of
my friends had a job out of college, and the fact that I didn't
made me feel like a failure. I thought graduation was going to
be the start of my life, but I felt in limbo. When was it going
to be my turn? I'd fought my depression like hell to get to
graduation, but someone moved the goalpost.

I thought Macon was bad, but not even having a place to
call my own felt even worse. I was couch surfing, at my own
parents' house.

Moving back in with them felt like taking a step backwards in my journey to adulthood. They had moved recently; their house was in a new city, so I didn't have any local friends. I felt like I was supposed to be starting my life, but now I felt like even more of a kid than before. Where I was once free to make all decisions, I suddenly had a curfew and set of familial expectations that I hadn't had to live with for two years. I had grown and changed so much I felt cramped both physically and emotionally.

I felt like each day I didn't have a job I was being silently judged, even if they never said it out loud. Every question about how the job search was going was probing a sore spot. Since I'd been a good student, I'd assumed I would easily get a job lined up before graduation, but that wasn't the case. I hadn't thought to network before I moved to a new city. I'd just finished a momentous thing and felt like I was at square one. There was no celebration, only the new to-do list.

I'd been dealing with severe chronic depression the entire time in Macon, and I could feel myself dipping even lower as I desperately searched for a job. I felt like a leaf blowing in the wind with no roots to keep me grounded. I was tired of constantly feeling like I was in between phases of life but never with both feet planted in the moment.

So, I went back to therapy.

This was the same therapist that had walked me through my breakup with James. I sat in her office this time feeling so frustrated. In my head I felt like a caged animal with no way out, and I felt guilty for thinking that while my parents were providing for me during this transition. I wanted to feel grateful, but graduation felt like falling off a cliff with no safety net. I felt angry at the world and didn't know what to do with it.

The clock ticked on the wall as I sat between familiar yellow pillows.

"So, what can I help with today?" she asked.

"Since graduation, I moved back in with my parents and feel like we are speaking two different languages."

"That's understandable. That sounds like a natural part of growing up."

"In Macon I had freedom to do what I wanted, but now they've said they'd throw me out if I chose to sleep over with Cayden," I shared. "I feel like their love is conditional."

"Wait, how old are you?" she asked.

"Twenty-two."

"You're over the age of eighteen, and your sex life is none of their business. However, until you move out, your base level of the Maslow's Hierarchy of needs is dependent on them," she said. "So, while we won't compromise who you are as a person, you will have to find a way to compromise temporarily until you move out." I was surprised at her response, but thankful.

For most of my life it felt like what I did with my body was something my church and parents thought they were supposed to monitor and control. Sex and moving in before marriage were looked down upon.

So, my therapist proposed an interesting solution. She compared moving back in with my parents to visiting a foreign country.

"When you visit another country, for the most part, you try to be mindful of their social norms and customs," she said. "So, if you go to a Muslim country and wear a hijab, it is out of respect for where you are visiting, but it doesn't mean you have become a citizen or changed your religion."

She helped me realize that I could believe whatever I wanted; I didn't have to let them change that.

I knew in order to beat my depression that therapy wouldn't be enough to get through this rough transition. I needed to find community. Desperate, I returned to the one thing I had been taught to turn to, even though personal experience had told me not to. I was going to give church one more chance to work for me like I had been promised it would.

Sermons for young adults at this church were held at a bar, and I thought it was so innovative. It made it feel casual. Maybe this would be better. I could finally have a positive church experience.

A month into trying this group, a speaker was talking about why it is so important to show up in the church. We must practice being our authentic selves. Then, he took questions. I rose my hand before my brain could register that it was moving. *What am I doing?* I considered putting my hand down but at that point he was mid-sentence.

"Yes, the woman in the back with the purple shirt." The speaker pointed at me, and someone rushed over to give me a mic. *I guess this is really happening.*

"Okay, this is great and all, but I've been in small groups where when I did show up, I was told to shut up and sit down. When I asked difficult questions, I was handed books about why Christianity was the superior religion and articles about why certain pastors I resonated with were heretics." Speaking was excruciatingly difficult. I gripped the table, preparing for his rejection. "I am actually in this small group as a last-ditch effort to give church one more try, but I am so exhausted and have been hurt so deeply over and over and it sucks. What do you have to say to people like me?"

"First," he said. "On behalf of the church, let me apologize for the harm done to you. It was wrong. We need people like you to call us out so we can do better. So, thank you for being so honest."

"Thank you," I said between tears. I felt a small piece of hope grow. Maybe this time it would be different. He finished answering other questions and the night ended. My small group came around me in a circle and hugged me. "We want to hear your voice Natalie! Thank you for being so brave," they said. "We love you. We won't be like that; it was just one experience."

I wanted to believe them. But I'd come to hear that phrase a lot: "Don't make the one bad experience with the church reflect on the whole idea itself." The thing is it is never just one bad experience for people like me.

Michael Walrond Jr., pastor of the First Corinthian Baptist Church in Harlem, talks about religious trauma syndrome. You won't find this condition in the Diagnostic and Statistical Manual of Mental Disorders, which clinicians use to make their diagnoses. But the term has been gaining currency with psychotherapists, counselors, and others who work with people who are recovering from the harmful effects of religious indoctrination. Some churches "weaponize scripture and religion to do very deep damage on the psyche," he says.[39] Gay, lesbian, and trans people are told God condemns them, unwed mothers told they are living in sin, and many natural human desires are deemed evil.

A survey by the Trevor Project found that religious-based family rejection was the single most important common

---

39 Richard Schiffman, "When Religion Leads to Trauma," *New York Times*, February 5, 2019.

factor in LGBTQ+ youth depression, suicide attempts, and homelessness.[40] The teachings I grew up with made me feel sick, depressed, terrified, and doomed. Growing up internalizing not just shame and rejection, but divine damnation, we have to overcome toxic indoctrination on many levels and in many layers.

It didn't take long. My third meeting in, the illusion was shattered.

I sat in a booth at the bar, squeezed between girls spewing nonsense about people being traumatized into homosexuality. Nods of approval egged one another on to continue with proclamations of who they believed would be banished to a fiery eternity. I sat on my hands, my eyes staring down at my thighs, forcing myself not to move. Not to make a scene. If only they knew who sat amongst them.

Driving home from that meeting I called Janelle in a frenzy.

"Janelle...I need to vent."

"Okay, hit me, what's going on? Are you okay?" she asked.

"Not really. That small group. They were saying the shittiest things about the LGBT community and people who didn't call themselves Christians all going to hell. I can't even," I said, raising my voice as I released my anger. "I can't believe I didn't say anything. I am so mad at myself. I should've told them how offensive it all was. They didn't even know they were talking about someone like me. There was no consideration that anyone in the room might fit the exact demographic they were discussing."

"I know you've been struggling with deciding whether or not to stay. There's a fine line I've been trying to walk

---

40 "National Survey on LGBTQ Youth Mental Health 2020," Trevor Project, accessed February 12, 2021.

as your friend to support you, but I need to say I think it's time to move on," she said. "You have given them plenty of chances to prove you wrong, Nat. You've outgrown this part of your life. It's time to seek your people somewhere else. You deserve better."

"Yea..." I said, taking in my disappointment. I was so sure if I just gave church one more try that it might finally work for me. I was so angry something that framed itself as comforting and inclusive felt like a dagger in the heart. The more I leaned into my true identity, the more distant I felt from religion. It just didn't align with who I wanted to become.

I was ready to move out and create a life that felt more affirming. I was tired of having to conform to everyone else's expectations and couldn't wait for the freedom.

Looking for jobs out of college was hard. The positions that seemed like a good fit required a minimum of five years of experience, and the entry level ones seemed to always be scams. Each job fair was a cacophony of job seekers. When I'd almost given up, a friend told me to check a local job fair. I wanted to just stay home and sleep, but I threw on a suit, grabbed a few resumes, and drove to the building.

When I arrived at the job fair, I went from booth to booth, but no one was looking for someone in communications or marketing. As I wound my way through each hall, I was becoming more and more discouraged. *Was this going to be another waste of time?*

The last table I visited had a man in a blue suit with a big smile across his face.

"Hey there! Have you ever thought about working for a state agency?" he asked, waving me over.

"No, not really," I said. "I've been looking for a marketing or advertising agency."

"We have jobs in public affairs! Have you ever considered that?"

"What does that mean exactly?"

"People in our public affairs office oversee our press releases, interact with the media, and manage our website and graphic design. Stuff like that," he said.

"I have a ton of experience with writing, graphic design, and website management!" I said, starting to feel hopeful.

"Let me see your resume. We just had a position open up, but it closes at the end of the week." I exchanged my resume for his business card. "I'll be sure to pass it on to our director."

"Wow, thanks," I said, shaking his hand. I walked back to my car in a daze.

I didn't want to get ahead of myself, but something in my gut knew this was the next thing I wanted to pursue. When I got home, I prepared my portfolio website and sent in an application.

After four rigorous interviews, I got the job.

That position was the first step to regaining my confidence. I started to believe that maybe there was a place for me where I could shine.

COACHING QUESTIONS
- When have you felt in limbo before?
- Have you returned to a prior situation from your life and found that it does accommodate you as much as you remember?
- When have you struggled choosing between childhood upbringing and inner wisdom?
- Have you experienced religious trauma or felt like you didn't belong in the belief system that you were brought up in?

12

ADULTING

---

*"That horrifying moment when you're looking
for an adult and realize you are the adult."*

ANONYMOUS

When the pizza arrived, the delivery man had the patience
of a saint as eight-year-old me plopped on the entryway floor.
Our new puppy licked at my face. Each quarter, nickel, and
dime went "skrrrrreee" on the linoleum as I counted them
to prove I had enough. My family had been debating what
to have for dinner, and I was determined to have pizza. Dad
asked, "With what money?" and I offered to pay with my
chore money, a jingling Ziplock full of change.

We have pictures of this whole encounter. I still laugh at
my eyes bulging in amazement as the deliveryman handed
me the large pizza box that was almost as big as me. The
bouncing pigtails and bright eyes make me look like Boo
from *Monsters Inc*. My hands reached around both sides of
the heavy box as a huge grin spread across my face. Because

to me, it wasn't just a pizza. It represented freedom and power. I used my "hard-earned" money to get something. My parents had recently filed for bankruptcy and our world had turned upside down. I didn't know what bankruptcy truly meant. At eight years old, it meant having to play with hand-me-down toys and move to an unsafe neighborhood far from my old friends. We stopped eating out every other day, and it became a luxury that we had once in a blue moon. So that pizza was a rare treat I savored.

When I was in middle and high school and heard girls in the locker room complain about how their dad didn't buy them a $40,000 new car for their sixteenth birthday or their boyfriend didn't buy them an expensive bracelet for Valentine's Day, I felt alienated from them. I viewed money completely differently.

Fifteen years after the pizza story, my parents had been out of debt for a few years. But, even as a twenty-three-year-old the experience of bankruptcy stuck with me. I vowed to never have debt of my own, and this made me even more weird compared to my peers. My own bank account began to fill as I learned the ropes at my new job, dreaming of starting my life as an adult. Financial literacy was something my family had learned the hard way growing up. Now, I was budgeting for my move into my own apartment and saving an emergency fund so that I didn't go through the same pain.

I didn't recognize how progressive the idea was for a woman to have full control over her money. Women have been legally able to open their own bank accounts just in the last fifty years, since 1971.[41] I'll never forget the first time

---

41   Don Evon, "Could Women Not Do These 9 Things in 1971?," *Snopes*, September 3, 2019.

I learned the origin of "Mrs." was "Mr's." As in the possessive. Two hundred and fifty years ago, a woman became her husband's property when they married. She was no longer even considered a citizen. All she owned became her husband's. The Woman's Rights Petition to the New York Legislature in 1854 began to challenge this thought process.[42] Measures like this deeply upset tradition; they suggested that women were equal to men and did not naturally desire subordination.

It's strange to think the freedom I was preparing to transition into was something fairly recent in history that I took for granted. It was inherently controversial to have so much control over my fate as a woman.

At first, my new job made me feel like I was starting to become a "real" adult. I had a parking decal, my own office, and a lot of responsibility. But there were moments when I felt like a kid in a suit playing make-believe. Although I'd passed the rigorous interviews for a job that wanted someone with five or more years of experience, I still felt like an imposter. This fear was something I kept close to my chest as I continued to try to navigate this messy transition into adulthood.

Adolescence encompasses elements of biological growth and major social role transitions, both of which have changed in the past century. Earlier puberty has accelerated the onset of adolescence in nearly all populations, while understanding of continued growth has lifted its endpoint age well into the twenties.[43] In other words, we aren't taking on the traditional

---

42 "Woman's Rights Petition to the New York Legislature, 1854," Furman University, accessed February, 19, 2021.

43 Susan M. Sawyer, "The Age of Adolescence," *The Lancet: Child and Adolescent Health* 2, no. 3 (2018): 1.

obligations (parenting, buying homes, and investing in the future) that our parents did. Which makes it easy to feel like a fraud of an adult.

Moving day was a blur. I organized all the boxes and furniture for the movers to pack into their truck. It took them fifteen minutes. After we moved in all my stuff, my family and I went to a local restaurant. As we finished eating, I took my parents' house key off my key ring and slid it over to my dad. He looked at me with an exaggerated frown, and I hugged him as we both realized our relationship was about to permanently change. We were transitioning from a parent-child relationship to an adult-adult relationship, and after today I'd be taking responsibility for my own well-being.

My parents dropped me back at my new home, and I locked the door behind me. *This is it, no turning back now.* Boxes littered the floor, and most of the couches and other furniture were still wrapped in plastic. This was the only apartment I could find within my budget; everything else I'd found was almost double the rent. It was a small place, but I looked forward to decorating it. If I couldn't make this work, I'd have to move back in with my parents. *Welcome to adulthood.*

Life was moving so fast that I was having trouble landing with both feet in this moment. My brain felt like a hamster on a wheel, wasting a bunch of anxious energy without moving anywhere useful. This apartment was the thing I'd been working towards. I'd finally "arrived" again—I'd been miserable in Macon and at my parents' house, but now I had my own place. *Why wasn't I more excited?*

I was scared. This was my first real adult expense.

The clock said it was well past midnight, but I felt like it was four in the afternoon. I wrapped the covers around me and tried to go to sleep.

What if you have a random medical expense?

Or a fire burns everything you own?

Or you total your car again?

A neighbor started yelling loudly in the breezeway, and the commotion scared me.

Why were you trusted to get your own apartment?

Suddenly, I felt like a lost thirteen-year-old again, uncertain of who I wanted to be and what I was going to do with my life.

It finally struck me that one of the main reasons I was finding it difficult to nod off, besides my anxiety, was that my room smelled funny. Not dirty, but it was lacking the warm presence of home. Nothing was set up yet, and it felt like sleeping in a very strange empty hotel. Even my mattress, sheets, and bed frame were brand new. It was all foreign.

Most of my belongings were still in boxes, but I rifled through a few until I found a lavender candle. The bright flame danced as it filled my room with calm. I searched for some of my crystals and oracle cards and placed them on my nightstand.

My little sanctuary was coming together.

This was my chance to build something authentic. A place where I could be myself and cultivate my own joy and peace as an adult. Earplugs squished into my ears, and finally, sleep began to fall over my body.

That's a little better.

COACHING QUESTIONS

- In what ways, if any, do you still feel like a kid in your life?
- How has your parent-child relationship evolved? Either with your own parents and/or kids if you have them.
- When was the moment you realized you were the adult in your life, and how did it make you feel?
- In what ways are you neglecting becoming the adult in your life?

13

GEEK GIRLS

———

"The only way to make sense out of change is to plunge into it, move with it, and join the dance."

ALAN WATTS

The morning sun bounced around his office walls through the large window behind the desk. You could see the glowing gold dome of the Georgia capitol building a few streets down. My computer sat on the conference desk with the annual report pulled up on the screen. Seated side by side, I was presenting the new designs and asking for his feedback. My new boss interrupted me mid-sentence.

"Do you drink?" It caught me completely off guard. Wasn't this a work meeting? Also, why did he just interrupt me to ask me that of all things? I didn't like to drink, but he was the new boss; I wasn't sure what to say.

"Why?" I was suddenly very aware of his office door being closed, which had never bothered me before.

"It just looks like you could use one," he said, looking me up and down.

Did he just allude to me being uptight? Was that his version of flirting? What the hell is this?

I was incredulous and didn't know what to say next, so I kept presenting like he hadn't even interrupted in the first place. He didn't attempt to finish the conversation. When I sat down in my office after the meeting, I started to collect my thoughts and realized just how uncomfortable he'd made me. *Why hadn't I said anything?* I should have just told him he was making me uncomfortable. *Do I need to loosen up more?*

A month after I'd moved into my new apartment, my work had a reorganization. I'd learned a lot from my first boss and was sad to see her go. Our team seemed to have just hit a stride, and then it imploded. There had been so much change in my life in the past few years, so I was angry that more things were in flux.

It was even more frustrating that her replacement seemed to have significantly less managerial and communications experience. He was in his late twenties and much more laid back than most directors I'd met. Now, I was the only woman in the department and started to notice all the ways I was treated differently. However, it was my first job, and I didn't want to rock the boat. So, I did my best to accept the transition.

After reaching out to trusted friends, I was convinced to stick it out, despite my bad feeling. After a month of condescension and flirtation, I finally couldn't stay silent anymore.

Deadlines were important to me because I managed several large projects, and I depended on his input to move on to the next phase. There were several times that deadlines weren't met, and I pointed that out to him. Then, in a meeting, he casually said "Well, Natalie's over here yelling at me about deadlines." The three other men at the table chuckled, and my cheeks grew hot. Even though I'd wanted to yell at him, I knew I'd made a simple request. I looked around the room. The team never had a problem with the work I produced, but they did have a problem standing up for me/up to my boss. Each meeting I watched to see if he'd make fun of anyone else, but he didn't.

Ever since my first boss left, I'd been overwhelmed with the amount of work on my plate. We finally hired a new graphic designer, and I took her out to lunch on her first day, relieved to have another woman on the team. At the end of our meal, she paused and looked at me.

"Hey, can I ask you a question?" she said. "Promise you won't get offended?"

"Sure, what's up?" I grabbed my tray as we walked over to the trash can across the room.

"I hope this isn't weird...but are you bi?"

"Yes, I am! How could you tell?"

"I am too! You just have the vibe, but I wasn't sure." We walked into the elevator. The seven lit up, and it rose to our floor.

"Well now I am super hyped to have a fellow LGBT member in the office!" I adjusted the purse on my shoulder, taking in the good news. Maybe I could be more myself on this team with her here.

"Me too! But we can't talk openly about it," she said.

"Why not? I was planning on having a pride flag in my office in June."

"During my interview, our boss found my YouTube channel with my girlfriend," she said. "He suggested that I didn't bring it up at work."

"He said that during an interview..." My stomach fell. *You have got to be kidding me.*

The highlight of leaving Macon was that I could be comfortable being out again; I wasn't going to shove myself back in the closet. My head started spinning. There are not currently federal workplace protections for employees who are discriminated against based on gender identity and sexual orientation. If this job had the audacity to explicitly tell someone not to talk about a part of their identity, then I was done. I didn't want to risk someone firing me for being myself.

While I was evaluating my new job, I knew I had to find community quickly. In Macon, my depression caused me to become an antisocial hermit, and I wasn't going to let it steal my social life again.

Since church was no longer an option, I searched for groups that were aligned with what I wanted, a group of other nerdy and/or LGBT people who I could just be myself around. I found two groups that intrigued me: PFLAG and a local Meetup called Geek Girls of North Atlanta.

PFLAG is the United States' first and largest organization uniting parents, families, and allies with people who are lesbian, gay, bisexual, transgender, and queer.[44] During my first meeting, we all went around in a circle and shared our name and why we were there. When it got to my turn, I shared my name and that I was pansexual. Glancing around the room, I looked for the horror I'd seen in Charlotte's eyes years ago. When the leader of the PFLAG chapter opened their mouth, instead of asking to talk to me after the meeting, they accepted me exactly as I was with open arms. It was everything I'd wished church groups could have been. Being met with so much love and support was surreal and

---

44 "About PGLAG," PFLAG, accessed February 24, 2021.

healing. Most of the adults at these meetings were parents of trans children; their raw honesty was refreshing. They shared their struggles and wins as if it were natural. Going to a local chapter meeting was emotional because I got a peak behind the curtain of the local LGBTQ youth.

The Geek Girls group had a few different events including a biweekly trivia night at a local pizza place. My social anxiety got in the way for the first month until finally I jumped in my car and made myself drive there.

The smell of garlic and pizza dough wafted through the room as I walked into the Mellow Mushroom. A waitress came up to me, and I asked where trivia was being held. She smiled and pointed towards the balcony area. I pushed open the glass doors and steeled myself for awkward conversations.

Panic set in as I realized I'd have to look at each table as I struggled to identify faces I'd only seen on the Meetup app. Luckily I was able to eliminate any tables with men and found a table with five women sitting. One of them was working on a sewing project; it looked like a Victorian cosplay outfit. Another one was needle felting a small orange fox figurine. This looked like the right spot.

"Hey, is this the Geek Girls table?" I said, scanning their faces for confirmation.

"Yes! Have a seat." The woman with spiky purple hair holding the fox pulled out the seat beside her. "I'm Rachel! What's your name?"

"Hi Rachel! I'm Natalie." I scooted into the chair and glanced at a menu.

"So, what are your geeky obsessions?" Rachel asked. "You're new right?"

"I am." I searched my brain for what I felt comfortable sharing. "I love Harry Potter, reading books, and playing video games."

"Nice! What video games do you play?" This should be a simple question, but my brain reached a limit for new social interaction and completely blanked. My face grew more confused as I searched for an answer, feeling embarrassed. I probably looked like an imposter.

"Oh, uh, I am blanking on the names. I play a lot of looter shooters."

"Cool! When you think of the names, let us know," Rachel said. "Maybe we can get a group together and play sometime!"

"Sure!" Having another woman ask me about my nerdy side was an unexpected joy. I felt seen.

I ordered food and continued observing the group. It was odd. I couldn't place it, but this group instantly felt like home where church small groups had felt like a cage. Then it hit me. They aren't wearing masks, pretending to be perfect.

That's what it was...they just showed up and said what was on their minds instead of first filtering it to see if it was "Christian" enough. It was relieving to be in a group that was there to have fun, not be judgmental.

This group gave me the confidence to reembrace my inner nerd that I'd kept hidden away for years. The teen girl in me who got rejected from robotics club felt scared to admit she wanted to learn how to play video games and Dungeons & Dragons. Maybe it was too late; I'd missed my chance.

When I was in high school my dad, sister, and I would play Battlefield on our PCs, and I'd been envious of the guys that had Xboxes. Even though I played computer games I felt like consoles were reserved for guys. Which is funny because adult female gamers have unseated boys under the age of eighteen as the largest video game-playing demographic in the United States.[45]

When Cayden and I bought an Xbox console to celebrate my first birthday in the new apartment, I felt like a bit of an imposter. He introduced me to *Borderlands 2* as one of my first games. The cartoonish zombies with gas masks on ran at me with their limbs flailing yelling unintelligible phrases like "It's time for the meat puppet!" and "They told me to bring a pail lunch...you look pale enough to me!" I knew it was just a game, but I was keeping a full-blown panic attack at bay. It wasn't meant to be horror, but satire. My character died for what felt like the fiftieth time. Not only were the zombies overwhelming me, but there were so many buttons and sticks to manage on the controller. I was struggling with the hand-eye coordination.

"I hate this. I'm no good at it." I tossed the white controller on the bed with a huff.

"Relax, babe. It's a video game," Cayden said, watching me struggle with the controller. "It's part of learning."

Being good at things was something I'd tied so close to my identity; it was uncomfortable to be a newbie at something. I started to play games on my own, without Cayden there, and began to gain some confidence. I realized I'd been holding myself back from doing things I was curious about simply because I hated that "beginner" feeling.

I'd been feeling it a lot since I graduated. I started my first big girl job in October, and the thought of leaving was terrifying because I had new adult responsibilities. The following March I had just moved into my first apartment. I was only

---

45 Charles Pulliam-Moore, "Women Significantly Outnumber Teenage Boys in Gamer Demographics," PBS, published Aug 21, 2014, accessed February 24, 2021.

just starting to make new friends outside of church. And I was struggling with previously held beliefs that things like PFLAG and D&D were "evil." Everything felt new, and that was equal parts liberating and terrifying.

After some deliberation, I recognized that my job was no longer a good fit. It felt like a "boy's club," and I wanted to be treated as part of the team. Listening to my inner compass was a difficult decision. Staying meant compromising my identity just to make other people comfortable. Deciding where to define my boundaries and what I was willing to risk to establish them was difficult. I started applying for something new and tried to keep an open mind. Within a month I had an offer to work in the marketing department at a university that was five minutes away from my apartment. The new job felt like night and day.

It had a training where faculty and staff could learn all about the LGBT community and how to make it a safe environment for faculty, staff, and students who were queer. I was able to come out to my coworkers and meet many other LGBT people. With a new job, friends, and hobbies it felt like I was finally coming home to myself.

COACHING QUESTIONS

- Has "the beginner feeling" ever stopped you from doing something new?
- How do you decide acceptable boundaries for yourself even in a situation where you are inexperienced and uncertain?
- Explore a situation where you didn't want to "rock the boat." What did you consider when deciding what to do next?

14

RADICALLY INCLUSIVE

"Here, God is not approached as an object that we must love, but as a mystery present in the very act of love itself."

PETER ROLLINS, *THE IDOLATRY OF GOD: BREAKING OUR ADDICTION TO CERTAINTY AND SATISFACTION*

When I spotted the pride flag whipping in the wind I was overwhelmed with hope. I pulled my jacket a little tighter as the wind bit at my nose. The service was starting in a few minutes, and many people were pulling into the parking lot and heading inside. Anxiety slowly trickled into my mind as I walked towards the building with them. I bit my chapped lip, and the claustrophobia of crowds hit me. *You're going to be fine; I promise.*

Even though the Christian church had caused me so much pain, there was still a piece of me that missed regularly attending services on Sundays. I craved a community that celebrated differences and discussed taboo topics. So, when I read Emerson

Unitarian Universalist (UU) Congregation's vision statement, I wanted to learn more. They claim to be a radically inclusive, open minded, beloved community that is a vibrant source of peace, hope, and healing.[46] I'd been fed a similar narrative before, but I loved that Unitarian Universalism does not require an unchanging set of beliefs. Rather, they believe faith to be a spiritual journey that will last our whole lives. Their common ground is a respectful embrace of spiritual diversity. This was something that I wanted to learn more about.

A woman with thick black glasses and a bright green and pink scarf greeted me with a smile and handed me a bulletin with this Sunday's schedule. The old auditorium was large, with a wooden stage at the front, colorful paintings hung on the walls, and rows of chairs with back-pockets that held songbooks. It felt traditional, which gave me pause. *Why do you believe this is going to be different?* But as soon as I heard the Tibetan singing bowls, Buddhist prayer, and female minister, I was hooked. The service was radically eclectic.

Compared to the last group that thought people of other faiths were going to hell, this was a breath of fresh air. At the end of the service, the minister shared they would be having a Thanksgiving potluck. I'd been planning on heading straight home but felt my curiosity peak. I could meet some of these people and get to know them more if I stayed.

"Hey! I haven't seen your face before," the older gentleman sitting next to me said. "I'm Pete, you should stay for lunch!"

"Hi, I'm Natalie," I said, shaking his hand. Most of the room was moving upstairs for the meal. "I was just trying to decide if I would stay. I don't do great with crowds."

---

46 "About Us: Our Vision and Mission," Emerson UU Marietta, accessed January 26, 2021.

"You'd love it! Everyone makes their best food." He rubbed his hands together in excitement.

"Alright, you've convinced me." He and I walked towards the stairs together.

I grabbed a plate of food as the line snaked around to several tables with turkey, ham, tofu, and any Thanksgiving side you could possibly imagine. As I stood in line the woman in front of me asked me how I was doing.

"It's my first time here," I said. "I really enjoyed the service."

"Wasn't it wonderful?" she said, guiding me over to one of the foldout tables. "You should come sit with me. I'll introduce you to everyone."

As people gathered around, I learned that she was the head of the congregation's Immigration Justice task force. She told me that groups of people from their community would help immigrants find lawyers who were dealing with ICE. They distributed "Know Your Rights" cards in Latino communities. Both the Cobb County Pro-Immigrant Alliance and the Georgia Latino Alliance for Human Rights were partners with this community.

I was struck by how involved these people were with people in need. In any Christian church I'd been in, there was a lot of talk about feeding the hungry and being inclusive. Yet we only had one week a year where we actively focused on being out in the public. This was such a contrast.

"That's amazing." I dug into my plate of food. "I noticed the pride flag out front, so do you work with the local LGBT needs as well?" I wanted to test the waters and see if this really was as inclusive as they said.

"Oh! We have an LGBT Justice task force that actively lobbies and participates in town hall discussions."

"Wow! Well, I'm pansexual, and I'd love to learn more."
Did I just come out to strangers? I pinched my arm under the table to make sure I wasn't dreaming. No one batted an eyelash or interrupted me to talk about this later. She just responded as if I'd told her my favorite color was purple.

"You should get involved! We always need more hands on deck," she said. "We just had a Transgender Inclusions in Congregations workshop this past week." *Where has this place been all my life?*

I nearly dropped my fork. *Could I be myself here?*

"What about a pagan community?" I asked, getting more excited.

"We have monthly moon circle meetings, and they meet for every festival on the Wheel of the Year!" she shared. "We also have a weekly Buddhist sitting circle and Qi Gong practice."

My head spun, and I wondered if I'd been introduced to an alternate universe. They actively held space to show up authentically in a way I'd never experienced in a congregation. It was an invitation to be curious instead of being labeled as a rebel.

We finished the meal, and when I got back to my car, I had to sit for a moment and drink it all in. This morning had started with a lot of uncertainty, but this was more than I'd bargained for.

Growing up, religion felt like a checklist that dominated a lot of life. If we went to church, we were good; if we didn't, we were bad.

Were you baptized?

Had you prayed today?

Did you give your tithe to the church?

Have you kept yourself a virgin?

It felt like appearance mattered above all else, and when people chose vulnerability they were shunned. As long as you appeared to be checking off the items on these lists, it didn't matter what you did with the rest of your life. The Christian church had acted as the arbiter and gatekeeper of divinity. I wanted to be around people who were inquisitive, not who were preoccupied with looking good.

One of the most compelling pieces of research I found when exploring religion was in *Letter to a Christian Nation* by Sam Harris. He says this:

> "While believing strongly, without evidence, is considered a mark of madness or stupidity in any other area of our lives, faith in God still holds immense prestige in our society. Religion is the one area of our discourse where it is considered noble to pretend to be certain about things no human being could possibly be certain about. It is telling that this aura of nobility extends only to those faiths that still have many subscribers. Anyone caught worshiping Poseidon, even at sea, will be thought insane."[47]

I had been told by the church that people who left religion and forsake their faith turn to drugs and alcohol. It seems like people in the church think skeptics are immoral people who just want to sin. But I've been freer than ever to just love people and really value every interaction I have. Not believing in an afterlife has freed me to be present in the moment and to love each person that I come across. It's given me a greater sense of responsibility for the people around

---

47   Sam Harris, *Letter to a Christian Nation* (New York: Alfred A. Knopf, 2006), 23.

me because this life is the one that we need to make good. Ironically, I think becoming an agnostic atheist has made me a better Christian.

I view all my spiritual practices as a psycho-spiritual drama that I put on for myself for the purpose of healing and inspiration. Whether it is reiki, Christianity, witchcraft, pagan traditions, or Buddhism, there are powerful archetypes that I can learn from and call upon when I need more of that energy in my life. I believe nothing is true and everything is sacred. All religions are made up and only have the power we give to them. So why not have fun with it and do something that feels empowering?

When it comes to religion, I don't feel the need to label myself as anything in particular. When I released all the things I was told I "should" believe, a lot of my anxiety went away with too. I no longer had to hide parts of myself to make other people more comfortable. I choose to listen to a wide variety of Christian, pagan, and atheist voices because I want to be part of a human experience. I'm most interested in inclusive empathy.

Growing up in Christianity and the church made me feel isolated and fragile. Now, I lean into what makes me feel alive and grounded and I don't worry about what other people think about it. Because, in the end, spirituality and religion is a tool to help us make sense of the world and who we want to become.

COACHING QUESTIONS
- What family traditions were passed down to you? Are they still serving you?
- What rituals or habits help you feel grounded?
- Is your current belief system working for you? Why, or why not?

15

AUTHORITY

—

"I think one of the defining moments of adulthood is the realization that nobody's going to take care of you...The fiction of continuity and stability that your parents have painted for you is totally necessary for a growing child. When you realize that it's not the way the world works, it's a chilling moment. It's supremely lonely. So, I understand the desire for someone to be in charge...No one is in charge. And honestly, that's even cooler."

ADAM SAVAGE, "FOOD FOR THE EAGLE"

When the day came to join the Zoom call, my body was humming with anticipation. I clicked the link, and there he was, relaxing on a lawn chair with a bright green hedge behind him. There were two other people in my group, and they shared first, each of us getting thirty minutes to work with Rob. I waited nervously while he chatted with another person, wondering what he would say to me.

Rob Bell had a huge influence on me when I was wrestling with how I wanted to show up in the world. When I lived in Macon, my dad had introduced me to this podcast called "You Make it Weird" by Pete Holmes. A recurring segment on the podcast was F.O.R.B's or "Friends of Rob Bell," where he interviewed people like Science Mike, Peter Rollins, and Richard Rohr—who all formed my understanding of religion during a struggle with mental health.

Now, he was about to coach me through the imposter syndrome I'd been struggling with. This past year I'd dropped out of a master's program in Positive Psychology to write my first book instead. Letting go of the traditional education route and pursuing this big dream made me uneasy. I was a beginner, and there was so much unknown before me.

My turn came, and he focused his attention on me.

"Hi Natalie!" he said, looking at me on the Zoom screen. "This is how we do it. We meet fascinating people, and we talk to them. So, wherever you want to go."

"I love it." I laughed sheepishly, a little starstruck but trying to keep it together. "I'm in a similar situation as the two people who you helped before me. I am in a pivot in my career and have a lot of different projects I am working on, but the biggest thing I am struggling with is imposter syndrome due to my age."

"So how old are you?"

"Twenty-four."

"You're fine. You are incredibly wise and have lots of years," he said. "Okay, talk to me. Keep going."

"I'm working on my first book, and the phrase that keeps coming up for me is that I am intimidated by the responsibility of showing up."

"Yeah. Why does this project matter for you?" he asked.

"I want to help other people figure out what I've figured out at twenty-four," I explained. "A lot of older people I've talked to have said they wish they knew what I knew at this age because their lives would have been quite different. I know if I don't show up and be vulnerable in this book, I won't be able to help people as deeply as I feel called to. I have to share what I know."

He pressed further, asking me to summarize what unique perspective I had.

"Through a lot of really difficult practice, I know what it looks like to function outside of traditional expectations and be okay with that," I replied.

"What kind of expectations? Name one for me," he said, his head cocked to the side with curiosity.

"Um...being debt free. Never having debt at all when people told me that it was impossible. I worked my way through college. I don't have any debt, and I won't, as far as I know, because that is a promise I've made with the universe."

"Aw! That is badass!" he exclaimed, looking at me with wide eyes and an even wider smile. "Okay. Did you notice right there, when you tell me that story, that there was no fear?" he replied. He went on to say that my 'Natalie' way of naming things worked perfectly. That I was just reporting what happened from my point of view.

"Yea, that is pretty cool," I realized.

"Now, notice your question was about being an imposter. But then older people wish they knew what you knew," he explained. "Okay, just for the record Natalie—and I think I speak for the committee here—if people are asking you how you know what you know and to do what you do, that is the opposite of imposter. That is someone who knows what's up."

His reassurance was comforting. He put words to something I couldn't verbalize before; people coming to me for help meant I was the exact opposite of an imposter. So why did I struggle with feeling like one?

In a March 2020 interview, Glennon Doyle said something that really stuck with me:

> "There is no right or wrong; there is no good or bad, except what you've been conditioned to," she said. "So, for example, when I was deciding what to do with my marriage, the feminist would tell me this was the right thing to do, the Christians would tell me this was the right thing to do, the parenting experts would tell me this was the right thing to do, and all of those things would be different."[48]

There are so many "right" ways to do things. We often aren't taught to be curious. For many of us, our sense of right and wrong comes from our family of origin. Breaking those traditions can be incredibly difficult.

It reminds me of a breakfast I had with my dad. Through the entire meal, my thoughts raced. The smell of bacon and fresh coffee filled the air, and I took a sip of my water. But it didn't do much for my parched throat that felt like sandpaper.

You have to tell him.

The waitress came over to our table, and I ordered another latte as I picked at my eggs and bacon.

You can't put it off another day, just say something.

My foot tapped quickly on the floor. There was loud pop music playing in the background, and multiple conversations

---

48 *Marie Forleo,* "Glennon Doyle Talks Marriage, Sexuality & Choosing an Untamed Life," March 9, 2020, video, 48:03.

being had at each booth. Plates and silverware clinked as other families enjoyed their food. I played with the zipper on my jacket, pulling it back and forth to try to calm down. *He's going to hate you.* The background noise jostled my brain even further and made it difficult to concentrate as my dad told me about the latest podcast he'd been listening to.

He and I had started a new tradition of getting brunch together once a month since I moved out. We always had a lot to talk about and would chat for hours. I usually enjoyed it since he and I had become so close lately, but today my stomach was in knots. I couldn't sit still. This time was so valuable to me, and I didn't want it to end. I kept running the possible results of the conversation over and over in my head, and all of them ended with him disowning me.

I'd moved in with Cayden a few months after moving out in my own.

My boyfriend and I had been dating long distance for three years, and he had recently graduated. We'd been talking about moving in together for months, but I still had reservations about how my parents would take it. I also wondered if we were ready for such a big transition, especially since Cayden didn't have a job yet.

My parents are pre-marital coaches at their church and discourage moving in before marriage. I wondered if they'd accept me as they had when I came out as pansexual. But this ran deeper. We didn't talk about the LGBT community growing up. But it was drilled into us from a young age to not have sex or move in with a partner—both by my parents and the church. Even though I no longer identified as Christian, parts of me still wrestled with the shame I was supposed to feel, but didn't. Wasn't I being a foolish person? I felt conflicted.

But today, I'd decided it was time to rip off the Band-Aid and tell my dad. If we were working on building a real relationship, I wanted it to be built on honesty. Yet, I couldn't spit the words out.

"Hey, you look a little distracted over there," my dad said across the booth. I looked up from playing with my food and met his eyes.

"Yeah, there's something I want to tell you, but I can't seem to get it out," I said as my fork clanked on my plate. It was getting harder to breathe, and I tugged at my scarf.

"Would you feel more comfortable in the car?" he asked.

"I think so. It's going to be hard either way, but the noise of this diner is getting to me."

He waved our waitress over and paid the bill. We walked to the car in silence. As soon as we sat down and closed the doors, I started crying.

"I can see that whatever this is, it's really hard for you," my dad said, putting a hand on my back. "Do you want me to wait a bit so you can calm down first?"

I nodded and blew my nose. He rubbed my arm, and I let it all out. A few deep breaths helped to slow my heart, and my thoughts began to organize.

"So, what do you want to tell me sweetie?" he asked. Looking at me with concern in his eyes. After what felt like half an hour of crying and not being able to just say it, I finally told him.

"Cayden and I moved in together, and I am so scared that you and mom are going to stop talking to me," I said.

He paused for a few minutes, taking it all in.

"I've been trying to figure out how to tell you guys," I said. "But I've been really scared, and I'm tired of feeling this way." The car was silent.

Why doesn't he just say something? I fiddled with my seat belt as I waited for his response, picking at a frayed string.

"Well, it seems like you value loyalty. Do you feel like you have that in this relationship?" he asked.

His question surprised me.

"Yes. We've been together for three years. He's my person," I answered.

"And he treats you well? You feel safe and respected?" he asked.

"I do."

"Well, you're an adult now. Your mom and I don't have to like your decisions. But we do love you, for who you are not what you do," he said.

I breathed a sigh of relief, realizing he was the same man who accepted me when I came out two years ago.

We hugged and sat in the quiet for a few moments before I said goodbye and opened the car door. I felt a barrage of different emotions. I was thankful he didn't want to cut off all communication and that he took my decision seriously. But I'm sure that the conversation was exhausting for him too. I was tired from how much effort it took to be honest with my dad. I was excited for the future, yet apprehensive.

While I didn't assume that living together would be easy, I definitely underestimated how challenging it would be to share a home with a partner. In the beginning, we were so happy to transition from being two hours away to moving in. Having a companion to share my life with was so comforting.

But we started fighting, a lot. Our fights would often lead to me taking a drive to go let out loud screams or scribbling furiously in my journal. They would start small; the trash not being taken out could easily serve as kindling to what would soon become a large fire, with me accusing Cayden of not listening or helping and Cayden pointing out my failure to communicate. Some of the worst fights lead me to question if my Dad was wrong and should have stopped me from moving in with Cayden.

It wasn't easy; but, we learned I was an auditory processor, and he was an internal processor. When I perceived him to be shutting down, he just needed space to think. I had to learn how to calm down, take a beat, and have a calmer conversation with him. After every fight, we sit down and discuss what could have gone better. We make sure the other person felt heard and apologize when necessary. He'd encourage me to be more direct and ask for what I wanted instead of alluding to it. Which is something I've never had a partner do before.

It was in stark contrast to when I dated James, and he wanted to silence me. Cayden and I were both dedicated to growing together, as a team. I go home because what's waiting for me is understanding and communication. Living with him was different than how I'd been told it would go.

A lot of life felt like this.

My generation was told to go to college, get a job, find a spouse, and buy a house. But life is never that simple.

I wish it had been made clearer how everyone's journey is vastly different. Instead of compliance, I wish they'd encouraged more curiosity. As I felt freer to ask myself what I wanted beyond the traditions set before me, my life started to change. I felt more confident to pursue my passions and stand strong in my decisions instead of looking for validation from people like my parents. I no longer believed myself an imposter. I became my own authority.

COACHING QUESTIONS

- Who is the authority figure in your head? Is it a parent, or is it you?
- When have you felt most supported in following your dreams?
- How have you handled decisions that went against your family of origin?
- What would it look like to accept that life hasn't turned out the way you imagined it?

16

REBUILDING

---

*"There is nothing stronger than a broken
woman who has rebuilt herself."*

HANNAH GATSBY, *NANETTE*

I swallowed my first little white pill with a gulp of water and
sat down on the tan loveseat in my living room.

Here goes nothing.

My journal was on my lap to take note of any changes,
and I adjusted the pillow behind my back. Will I even notice
a difference? I tapped the pen on the notebook as I waited.
The sun was peeking over the clouds, and the birds were just
starting to sing. I glanced out the porch window and began
to feel the shift.

My thoughts slowed.

My body's ever-present anxious energy quieted.

I was told it would take weeks to feel the full effects, and
I may not notice anything the first few days. But my depression had such a hold on my mind that even the first few
hours there was a significant change. The sludgy quicksand

of depression began to leave my mind, and I began to weep from the relief.

Part of facing my struggle of the recent move-in with Cayden was taking the time to address my physical and mental health. Three days earlier, in January 2020, I'd had my first doctor's appointment on my new insurance plan. There was a lot of typical paperwork including a depression screening. I answered honestly, but since I'd moved out on my own, I figured my depression had sorted itself out. I was less angry with the world and didn't feel as bad as I did in college. The problem was the circumstance, right?

During the routine checkup she asked me about the screening.

"You wrote that you struggle with feeling tired and sad at least one day out of the week," She took off the blood pressure cuff and made a note on her chart. "Have you considered medication?"

"As a last resort, but I've been managing fine without it." I eyed the ground.

"Well, can you describe the tiredness to me?"

"Some days, I wake up and it takes extra energy to get out of bed. I've had a brain fog for as long as I can remember, and some days it's just worse than others." My hands began to sweat. "But everyone gets into a funk once and a while, right?"

"Not quite like that." She looked at me and smiled. I appreciated her patience. "Would you be willing to try medication?"

"I've just been nervous about it changing my brain or personality permanently." I sat on my hands to distract myself. "I don't want to become dependent on something, and I seem to be getting along alright without it."

"I can understand that fear. Antidepressants like this don't really change your personality; they change your distress tolerance baseline," she explained. "If you struggle with depression, this is much lower than the average person. I just want to help you have more energy in your day-to-day."

"I guess I could try it." I said, warily.

I felt like if I took medication, I'd be cheating the system, like the stories I'd heard of kids taking an Adderall just to do better on a test. It's common to be bothered by the idea that you can't beat depression without medication. Some research says many people "think of antidepressants as a kind of crutch and think they would see themselves as being weak and helpless if they had to rely on them."[49]

Throughout the next few weeks, I felt everything shift just like when I got my glasses. The world felt more vibrant and exciting. My negative self-talk completely went away. I stopped hating on my body and calling myself lazy. I had more energy to socialize and pursue hobbies. There was a spring in my step. My emotions were easier to regulate, and I got in less arguments with Cayden and my family.

One of the biggest physical manifestations from my antidepressants was the change in my watercolor paintings.

I'd started to try watercolor when I first moved out on my own a little over a year ago. There was something about the surrender of power to the paint that was appealing to me. Perfectionism had been one of my core vices, and I wanted to break it by practicing one of the hardest types of paint to master.

When I began, I bought a kid's watercolor pallette and a set of brushes for five dollars. My first attempt was awful, and the colorful paints mixed on the page to create a muddy brown. I wondered if I made a huge mistake trying to take this on.

---

49   "Depression: Experiences with Antidepressants," Institute for Quality and Efficiency in Health Care (IQWiG), accessed January 30, 2021.

YouTube video tutorials saved the day. As my painting got better, I invested in nicer tools. I learned how to layer the paint to give the painting lifelike depth. When I started my antidepressants, I was able to translate the vibrant world I saw onto the page. Each sweeping stroke on the wet paper had a smudging quality that rendered the image watery, like a reflection in a rippled puddle. The bright colors mirrored my new reality, like a novel condensed onto a single page. I recognized the significance in the improvement of my paintings, but I didn't realize others would too.

"You started painting light and shadows that I didn't know you could do with watercolor," my dad said on our monthly FaceTime. Tears welled in his eyes, and he put his hand over his heart as he continued. "It's like I had the gift of seeing the world become more colorful for you; there was suddenly joy and depth in your paintings."

"I noticed the change too," I said, my voice breaking. "I feel more alive."

"It wasn't just your paintings that changed," he said. "The rapid pace of your evolution in 2020 has been astonishing as your dad. You seem more sure of yourself, like I'm finally getting to meet the real you."

"It's like something finally clicked, and I'm free to show up as my whole self instead of hiding behind a mask."

"I feel like you are leading me by example with your life lately. I want you to know that."

"Thanks, Dad." I smiled.

This conversation meant a lot to me because my relationship with my dad was so strained in middle school and high school. But as I grew up, I started having deeper conversations with him. Lately, I'd been able to talk to him about religion and spirituality. He'd even shared a few atheists that he looked up to; it seemed like his point of view of the world was expanding, just like mine had.

I felt lucky to be fully seen by him. He put words to the changes he saw in me, and it felt liberating.

Before I took medication, I didn't have the words to express that I had chronic depression for most of my life. I just assumed I was a moody teenager who had never quite outgrown that stage. My friends in high school and college talked about fighting through a brain fog, sadness, and a lack of energy. A lot of my peers were tired and dissatisfied with life.

Just like my glasses story, I thought everyone experienced this; it was just part of being human. I felt like I had to push through it but couldn't.

Part of me had always associated mental health with mental ability. If I was smart and praised in school, then how could I also have depression?

I was an intelligent woman, top of her class, and thought if I could just do enough holistic things, I could outsmart my darkness. I figured I'd done enough research online. I just needed to exercise, eat well, take vitamins, get enough sleep, commit to my hobbies, make friends, listen to affirmations and mantras, and do well in school, and THEN I'd be happy, right?

I just wasn't doing enough.

I just needed to care more.

If I could just get this routine ingrained in me, it would fix everything.

The problem was that trying to stay on top of all this took all my energy to function, and I didn't have much left over for anything else. The chronic depression had been stealing all my energy.

Not everyone's experience with medication works well like mine did. Many people assume that depression is easily identifiable, only manifesting as persistent sadness that doesn't lift. However, symptoms of depression can take a variety of forms. The American Psychological Association says "people with depression may experience a lack of interest and pleasure in daily activities, significant weight loss or gain, insomnia or excessive sleeping, lack of energy, inability to concentrate, feelings of worthlessness or excessive guilt, and recurrent thoughts of death or suicide." [50]

Research indicates that more cases of depression are characterized by the accrual of multiple chronic mild stressors, such as work-related stress, homemaking demands, and financial trouble than by major losses such as divorce or the loss of a job. [51]

Unfortunately, mental health is still a taboo subject in our culture, so I want to help normalize this discussion. Something like medication is seen as a last resort, or something to be avoided at all costs. It's sometimes a symbol of someone's moral failing. If depression was talked about in more detail at home, school and with doctors, I may have been able to get the help I needed much sooner. Instead, I assumed I was being ungrateful because I couldn't appreciate the life I already had.

Many people don't want to disclose anything for fear of being treated differently. Media tends to portray people with mental health issues as second-class citizens who are broken.

50   "Psychology Topics: Depression," American Psychological Association, accessed January 29, 2021.

51   Andrew Billings and Rudolph Moos, "Chronic and Non-chronic Uni-Polar Depression: The Differential Role of Environmental Stressors and Resources," *Journal of Nervous & Mental Diseases* 172, no. 2 (1984): 69.

There is evidence that replacing a "disability" or "illness" paradigm with a "diversity" perspective takes into account both strengths and weaknesses and the idea that variation can be positive in and of itself.[52]

Our curiosity about mental health could provide an opportunity for transformation. We will become better equipped to seek the help we need when we acquire the language to name it. Choosing to be brave and curious about mental health led me to be the woman I am today.

COACHING QUESTIONS

- Do you feel comfortable talking to your family and friends about mental health? Why or why not?
- What role has the discussion around mental health played in your own life?
- What are a few ways you can normalize these discussions?

---

52 Thomas Armstrong, "The Myth of the Normal Brain: Embracing Neurodiversity," *AMA Journal of Ethics* 17, no. 4 (2015): 350.

17

SPECTACLE

—

"Answers? Forget answers. The spectacle is all in the questions."

REBECCA GOLDSTEIN

When the world came to a halt in the spring of 2020, we were all forced to confront who we were without our busy lives and ambition. We were stripped of our achievement-oriented identities and overstuffed schedules and thrust into a highly uncomfortable state of limbo. Inhabiting a space that has no norms is simultaneously scary and filled with possibility.

We all yearn for transformation, but the current cultural conversation leads us to believe change is this incredibly positive and desirable experience. Our society makes metamorphosis sound easy. But the truth is, growing is slow, messy, difficult, and almost always painful.

In Glennon Doyle's book, *Untamed*, she writes, "Being human is not hard because you're doing it wrong, it's hard because you're doing it right."[53] Sometimes I forget this. I think that if I just work hard enough, then I can arrive at a place where everything is easy and makes perfect sense.

The pandemic made us sit still in the discomfort. It interrupted the stories we've been telling ourselves about who we are supposed to be. It removed the audience we've been performing for our entire lives and allowed us the space to consider what we actually want. We felt withdrawal from our productivity addiction. Suddenly, the curtain was pulled back, and we had a collective awareness of how our systems were failing us when we were too busy to pay attention. Now there is this tension because we know. We can't unsee it.

Instead of living life on autopilot, we get to slow down and observe the life we are in the middle of building. It's an invitation to take an active role in creating the life we desire.

We've been gifted a cosmic reset to build something new.

The pause caused by a global pandemic revealed the uncomfortable truth that there is no destination that we are headed towards, no plans we can actually make; there is only now. Any impending doom we might be feeling isn't about the past or future. It's about missing the present.

Regret is about the past, and anxiety is about the future. But, curiosity is about now, feeling an active presence in the world we inhabit.

We've started to recognize this screen-bound state of dis-association from our bodies and our planet.

We are having a collective "glasses" moment.

---

53   Glennon Doyle, *Untamed* (New York: Penguin Random House LLC, 2020), 50.

I hope that we can start replacing the old foundations of the past with something that is more inclusive. We must find another set of beliefs, values, and processes to take their place. We are being pushed to the edge of our core childhood wounds. We can't keep doing the same thing over and over and expecting a different result. Embracing curiosity invites the transformation and healing we seek.

We spend so much of our lives trying to make our parents proud of us, trying to get someone to love us, and trying to get society to tell us we are successful. And all along we were just looking for validation from ourselves.

We've been taught to run from the pain of uncertainty.

Part of being curious is admitting there are things we don't know and acknowledging there is room to grow. If we are seeking clarity on our future, we must be brave enough to ask the right questions. In order to experience the transformation we crave, we must face the questions we've been avoiding. Curiosity about where our beliefs come from helps us dismantle what isn't working anymore and build a new foundation.

What do I have?

What do I want?

Why do I want it?

How do I get it?

Deconstructing social norms as an individual is one thing, but creating a lasting cultural shift takes a dedicated community. Even now, amidst an isolating, global pandemic, we rely on each other and form communities for mutual support.

In an episode of the podcast *Unlocking Us with Brené Brown*, Jen Hattmaker said: "If we are waiting on systems to overturn themselves, we're just going to go to the grave in an unjust world. So, this work is ours to do."[54] We are radically imagining a future in which we are its architects and builders.

The world says, "this is the way it's always been done," but what if we leaned into possibility?

The world says, "accept abuse as love," but what if we choose to love ourselves first?

The world says, "shut up and sit down," but what if we find our voice and speak up?

The world says, "chase heteronormativity," but what if we love on a spectrum?

The world says, "it's all blobs of color," but what if we just need a new pair of glasses?

Thanks to curiosity, I got the help I needed and changed my life path. Whether it was getting out of an abusive relationship, leaving toxic theology, or managing my depression, my questions helped me come back home to myself again and again. I hope to help others find the same freedom. Instead of a career in marketing, I am now following my call to being a life coach. Being an excellent coach starts with this book and prompting the right questions, urging you to pick up your glasses.

Instead of being caught up in having all the right answers, let us enjoy the spectacle of embracing curiosity.

COACHING QUESTIONS

- What does it look like to let go of needing to know all the answers, and embracing curiosity instead?
- What will you let go of to let transformation happen?

---

54 Jen Hattmaker, "Longing, Belonging and Faith," April 21, 2020, in *Unlocking Us with Brene Brown*, produced by Brene Brown Education and Research Group, LLC, podcast, MP3 audio, 82:13.

- How can you use curiosity as your ultimate self-care tool?
- Explore how you want your life to look going forward.
- What if showing up is enough?

ALL COACHING
QUESTIONS

———

CHAPTER 1

- Have you been taught that certain questions/topics are off-limits?
- Are there areas of your life that you don't give yourself permission to be curious about?
- Explore your own metaphorical "glasses moments." How did these moments make you feel?
- When was a time that you questioned "the way things have always been done?"

CHAPTER 2

- Explore a time you abandoned yourself to fit in. How did it make you feel?
- Do you struggle with setting boundaries? Why or why not?
- What issues that you are struggling with now began in your childhood?

- How can you comfort and care for your inner child as an adult?

CHAPTER 3

- How would embracing sonder impact the relationships in your life?
- What questions can you ask in order to transform your relationships?
- Have you ever had a moment where you ignored a gut feeling? What happened?
- Have you ever changed yourself to fit in somewhere? What happened?

CHAPTER 4

- Have you hidden parts of yourself away for your own safety?
- What do you believe relationships are supposed to look like and where do those beliefs come from?
- How might you normalize conversations about the spectrum of sexuality?
- How has your curiosity been received by your community?

CHAPTER 5

- Explore a situation where you wanted to speak up, but you didn't.
- How do you determine what is true in your life?
- Do you have questions about your beliefs that scare you?
- Did you grow up with a certain set of beliefs? How did they affect you as you grew up?

CHAPTER 6

- Have you ever experienced an abusive relationship?

- What were the indicators that I was in an abusive relationship? What signs were there, if any?
- Consider if there are aspects of your life that you've accepted not because it's what you want but what you think is expected.

CHAPTER 7
- Do you struggle with codependency?
- Over the next few weeks make a note of the things you enjoy doing.
- Are aspects of your life that you've accepted not because it's what you want but what you think is expected of you?

CHAPTER 8
- Do you feel like you have a group of friends that understand you?
- Where might you look to find friends that share your interests?
- When was the first time you felt accepted by someone or a group of people?

CHAPTER 9
- Do you feel like you have a group of friends that understand you?
- Where might you look to find friends that share your interests?
- When was the first time you felt accepted by someone or a group of people?

CHAPTER 10
- Have you ever experienced a situation where you had to choose between what was right and what was easy?

- What signs help you navigate away from one priority (like fiscal responsibility) to focus on another one (like mental wellness or self-fulfillment), even if they're in opposition?
- What have you settled for in your past? What will you no longer settle for?
- When have you felt stuck? How did you get unstuck?
- Do you find people in your life (work/school/family) tell you to not "rock the boat" or "just go with the flow" because it would be inconvenient otherwise.

CHAPTER 11

- When have you felt in limbo before?
- Have you returned to a prior situation from your life and found that it does accommodate you as much as you remember?
- When have you struggled choosing between childhood upbringing and inner wisdom?
- Have you experienced religious trauma or felt like you didn't belong in the belief system that you were brought up in?

CHAPTER 12

- In what ways, if any, do you still feel like a kid in your life?
- How has your parent-child relationship evolved? Either with your own parents and/or kids if you have them.
- When was the moment you realized you were the adult in your life, how did it make you feel?
- In what ways are you neglecting becoming the adult in your life?

CHAPTER 13

- Has "the beginner feeling" ever stopped you from doing something new?
- How do you decide acceptable boundaries for yourself even in a situation where you are inexperienced and uncertain?
- Explore a situation where you didn't want to "rock the boat." What did you consider when deciding what to do next?

CHAPTER 14

- What family traditions were passed down to you? Are they still serving you?
- What rituals or habits help you feel grounded?
- Is your current belief system working for you? Why, or why not?

CHAPTER 15

- Who is the authority figure in your head? Is it a parent, or is it you?
- When have you felt most supported in following your dreams?
- How have you handled decisions that went against your family of origin?
- What would it look like to accept that life hasn't turned out the way you imagined it?

CHAPTER 16

- Do you feel comfortable talking to your family and friends about mental health? Why or why not?
- What role has the discussion around mental health played in your own life?
- What are a few ways you can normalize these discussions?

CHAPTER 17

- What does it look like to let go of needing to know all the answers, and embracing curiosity instead?
- What will you let go of to let transformation happen?
- How can you use curiosity as your ultimate self-care tool?
- Explore how you want your life to look going forward.
- What if showing up is enough?

EXTRA RESOURCES

CONNECT WITH THE AUTHOR
- Website (Join my email list for future books and courses): https://nsprz.com/
- LinkedIn: https://www.linkedin.com/in/nsprza/

LGBTQ+
- PFLAG: https://pflag.org/ (https://pflag.org/) - Founded in 1973 after the simple act of a mother publicly supporting her gay son, PFLAG is the nation's largest family and ally organization.
- Trevor Project: https://www.thetrevorproject.org/ (https://www.thetrevorproject.org/) - The Trevor Project offers accredited lifesaving, life-affirming programs and services to LGBTQ youth that create safe, accepting and inclusive environments over the phone, online and through text.
- Trevor Lifeline: (1-866) 488-7386 (tel: (1-866) 488-7386) - The only national 24/7 crisis intervention and suicide prevention lifeline for LGBTQ young people under twenty-five.

- TikTok Stand In Families - A Facebook Group to connect members of the LGBTQ+ community with stand in families for weddings and any other life events.

RELATIONSHIPS/ABUSE
- National Sexual Assault Telephone Hotline – (800) 656-HOPE (4673)
- Domestic Violence and Intimate Partner Violence Hotline – (1-800) 799-7233
- CoDependents Anonymous – https://coda.org/ - a program of recovery from codependence, where each of us may share our experience, strength, and hope in our efforts to find freedom and peace in our relationships with others and ourselves.
- Boundaries by Dr. Henry Cloud

MENTAL HEALTH
- National Alliance on Mental Illness (NAMI) Helpline – (800) 950-NAMI.
- Better Help: https://www.betterhelp.com/
- National Suicide Hotline: (800) 273-8255

A FEW OF MY
FAVORITE THINGS

BOOKS

- *Rage Becomes Her: The Power of Women's Anger* by Soraya Chemaly
- *Cassandra Speaks: When Women Are the Storytellers, the Human Story Changes* by Elizabeth Lesser
- *Big Magic* by Elizabeth Gilbert
- *Falling Upward* by Richard Rohr
- *The Dip* by Seth Godin

PODCASTS

- *Getting Curious* by Jonathan Van Ness
- *Tarot for the Wild Soul*
- *Akimbo* by Seth Godin
- *The Anthropocene Reviewed* by John Green
- *Dear Hank & John* by Hank and John Green
- *The Long and The Short Of It* by Pete Shepard and Jen Waldman
- *The Robcast* by Rob Bell
- *Unlocking Us with Brené Brown*

ENTERTAINMENT

D&D SHOWS
- *Critical Role*
- *Dimension 20*

VIDEO GAMES
- *The Witcher*
- *Destiny 2*
- *Borderlands 2 & 3*
- *Stardew Valley*

ACKNOWLEDGEMENTS

—

If you've made it this far, welcome. I am so honored that you chose to read my book. Becoming courageous enough to share my life, even the painful parts, took a lot of hard work. There were many moments I wanted to walk away from this project, and I am so proud of myself for finishing it. Thank you for taking the time to enjoy the fruits of that labor.

First, I want to thank my family—Mom, Dad, Katie, Nana, and Tata—for always encouraging me to be curious.

Charlie, my love, I believe you have earned a round of applause. You had a front-row seat to all the ugly crying, gnashing of the teeth, procrastination, and long nights needed to relive my experience and tell my story. There would be no book without your patience, love, and willingness to survive on takeout and frozen dinners for weeks. You kept me grounded.

Next, I'd like to thank Seth Godin, Taylor Harrington, Covington Doan, Stacy Richards, and everyone who had a hand in creating the Akimbo Emerging Leaders program. During commencement, I found the courage to take the leap and commit to writing my memoir. Without your program, there would be no book.

Genna, my best friend, who saw this book form before I wrote the first word, thank you for walking by my side through this journey since we met in DC.

Rob Bell's Something to Say workshop helped me break out of my imposter syndrome and realize my credibility comes from my lived experience. I'd like to thank him for coaching me through my fear.

I'd also like to thank Eric Koester, Brian Bies, Gjorgji Pejkovski, Aislyn Gilbert, and the incredible team I've had the honor to work with at the Creator Institute and New Degree Press. You helped redeem my 2020. Thank you for making my childhood dream of sharing my stories with the world come true.

I would also like to extend a huge thank you to my revisions and marketing editor, Joanna Hatzikazakis. Thank you for guiding my vision for this book and working with me on my chapters to realize this vision. I really appreciate you pushing me to dig deeper to tell the story that needed to be heard. Your encouragement helped renew my spirit and march on.

Thank you to Diane Haymes for taking awesome author profile photographs of me. You can check out her incredible work on her website at: https://www.dianehaymesphotography.com/.

Finally, this book was made possible also by a community of people who believed in me so fervently they preordered their copies and helped promote the book before it even went to print. Thanks to you all, many of whom read my early manuscript and gave input on the book title and cover. You are amazing, and as promised you are in the book:

Jason Marin
Jeff Brown
Viola Dwyer
Toku McCree
Kyle McGuffin*
Bliss Hendon
Erin Pace*
Gina Gareau-Clark
Leslie S. Esparza
Katherine Tindol*
Michele Reiner
Esmeralda Contreras
Dan Esparza*
Susana Zarazaga Soria
Danny van Leeuwen
Sam Miller
Stephen Ruaraidh Butler
Alisha Rodriguez
Hannah Duncan*
Tonya Parker
Bailey Rogg
Outi Leppanen
Gloria Dennard*
Allison Poon
Amanda Magdalenski*
Racheal Peters*

Elizabeth Johnson
Caroline Lazaro
Joanna Hatzikazakis
Genna Williams*
Eric Koester
Elaine Sweatman
Erin M. Van Liemt
Jennifer Gaar
Michael Chaffin
Mary Elizabeth Sheehan
Annemarie Fortier
Aarth Thakore
Charles Gaar*
Melissa Elaine le Fay
Mary Lou Monaghan
Linda McLachlan
Lindsey Brown
Geethika Koppisetty
Corey Bloes
Andrea Guzzo
Rachael Dean
Inmaculada Jimenez Lopez
Dave Oz
Ellie Parrish
Kelsey Waidhas

"In loving memory of Roswell Fredrick "Fred" Doty Sr. of Alpharetta, GA. A United States Navy veteran known for his honesty, generosity, and his devotion to his family and friends: September 5, 1935 - July 25, 2020."

*   extra donations or multiple copies purchased

APPENDIX

—

NOTE FROM THE AUTHOR:

Kibbe, Madora. "The Pot Roast Principle: Ask Questions—Even When You Think You Know the Answer." *Psychology Today,* February 8, 2014. https://www.psychologytoday.com/us/blog/thinking-makes-it-so/201402/the-pot-roast-principle.

Rohr, Richard. *Falling Upward: A Spirituality for the Two Halves of Life.* San Francisco: Jossey-Bass Inc., 2011.

Sterrett, David, Tom W. Smith, and Louise Hawkley. *Historic Shift in Americans' Happiness Amid Pandemic.* Chicago: NORC, 2020.

CHAPTER 1:

Burry, Madeleine. "This Mom Had No Idea Her Kids Were Struggling to See. Here's What She Wants Every Parent to Know." *Women's Health Magazine,* October 22, 2019. https://www.womenshealthmag.com/health/a29320512/child-vision-problems-personal-story/.

Pulley, Anna. "Ask Anna: During COVID-19 Pandemic, 32-Year-Old Surprised That He's Now Attracted to Other Men." *Chicago Tribune*, May 25, 2020. https://www.chicagotribune.com/redeye/ct-redeye-ask-anna-turning-gay-during-coronavirus-0528-20200525-oayama3bh5h45njkpuykgui4qy-story.html.

CHAPTER 2:

Chemaly, Soraya. *Rage Becomes Her: The Power of Women's Anger.* New York: Atria Publishing Group, 2018.

Cloud, Henry. *Boundaries: When to Say Yes, How to Say No to Take Control of Your Life.* Grand Rapids: Zondervan, 1992.

Dombeck, Mark. "The Long-Term Effects of Bullying." *American Academy of Experts in Traumatic Stress*, 2020. https://www.aaets.org/traumatic-stress-library/the-long-term-effects-of-bullying.

Hill, Catherine and Holly Kearl. *Crossing the Line: Sexual Harassment at School.* Washington, D.C.: AAUW, 2011.

CHAPTER 3:

Koenig, John. "Sonder." *The Dictionary of Obscure Sorrows* (blog). Oct 26, 2014. Accessed January 30, 2021. https://www.dictionaryofobscuresorrows.com/post/68194563177/sonder-n-the-realization-that-each-random.

Preidt, Robert. "Bullying Can Turn Victims Into Bullies." *Health Day*, May 1, 2016. https://consumer.healthday.com/

kids-health-information-23/bullying-health-news-718/bullying-can-turn-victims-into-bullies-710378.html.

CDC. "Suicidal Ideation and Behaviors Among High School Students — Youth Risk Behavior Survey, United States, 2019." Accessed February 5, 2021.

CHAPTER 4:

Boboltz, Sara, and Kimberly Yam. "Why On-Screen Representation Actually Matters." *Huffington Post,* Feb 24, 2017. https://www.huffpost.com/entry/why-on-screen-representation-matters_n_58aeae96e4b01406012fe49d.

CHAPTER 5:

Freud, Sigmund. *The Future of an Illusion.* Seattle: Pacific Publishing Studio, 1927.

Freud, Sigmund. *The Future of an Illusion.* Seattle: Pacific Publishing Studio, 1927.

State of Grace. "The Dark Reality Of Celebrity Endorsed Mega-Churches." July 13, 2019. Video, 11:45. https://youtu.be/KLuB-7fvMlhc.

CHAPTER 6:

Harvey-Jenner, Catriona. "A Shocking Number of Young Women Are in Abusive Relationships - but Many Don't Know the Signs." *Cosmopolitan,* May 9, 2018. https://www.cosmopolitan.com/

uk/reports/a20072270/domestic-abuse-relationships-cosmo-politan-uk-womens-aid-research/.

Womens Aid UK. "Why Don't Women Leave Abusive Relation-ships?" Accessed January 30, 2021. https://www.womensaid.org.uk/information-support/what-is-domestic-abuse/wom-en-leave/.

Punjaabi, Dimple. "The 7 Stages of Trauma Bonding." *The Mighty*, September 2020. https://themighty.com/2020/09/trauma-bonding-signs/.

CHAPTER 7:

Borenstein, Jeffrey. "Stigma, Prejudice and Discrimination Against People with Mental Illness." *American Psychiatric Association*, August 2020. https://www.psychiatry.org/patients-families/stigma-and-discrimination.

Co-Dependents Annonymous World. "What is Codependence?" Accessed January 30, 2021. https://coda.org/newcomers/what-is-codependence/.

Goffman, Erwin. *Stigma: Notes on the Management of Spoiled Identity*. New York: Simon & Schuster, 1963. Quoted in Rössler, Wulf. "The Stigma of Mental Disorders: A Millennia-Long His-tory of Social Exclusion and Prejudices." EMBO Reports 17, no. 9 (2016): 1250-1253. https://doi.org/10.15252/embr.201643041.

CHAPTER 8:

Basic Butch. "5 Reasons Coming Out Is Still a Big Deal." November 30, 2019. https://www.basicbutch.ca/single-post/2019/11/30/5-reasons-coming-out-is-still-a-big-deal.

Hurst, Biz. "Why 'Coming Out' Is A Way Of Life Rather Than A Moment In Time." *Huffpost*, October 14, 2013. https://www.huffpost.com/entry/coming-out-way-of-life-_n_4097732.

CHAPTER 9:

Bell, Rob. *Love Wins: A Book About Heaven, Hell, and the Fate of Every Person Who Ever Lived.* New York: HarperCollins, 2011.

Campbell, Joseph. *Hero With a Thousand Faces.* Novato: Pantheon Books: 1949.

Fowler, James. *Stages of Faith: The Psychology of Development and the Quest for Meaning.* New York: HarperCollins, 1978.

Shallcross, Lynne. "Validating the Quarter-Life Crisis." *Counseling Today*, April 22, 2016. https://ct.counseling.org/2016/04/validating-the-quarter-life-crisis/.

Zilca, Ran. "Why Your Late Twenties Is the Worst Time of Your Life." *Harvard Business Review*, March 7, 2016. https://hbr.org/2016/03/why-your-late-twenties-is-the-worst-time-of-your-life.

CHAPTER 10:

John Hopkins Medicine. "Integrative Medicine & Digestive Center: Reiki." Accessed February 17, 2021. https://www.hopkinsmedicine.org/integrative_medicine_digestive_center/services/reiki.html.

CHAPTER 11:

Schiffman, Richard. "When Religion Leads to Trauma." New York Times, February 5, 2019. https://www.nytimes.com/2019/02/05/well/mind/religion-trauma-lgbt-gay-depression-anxiety.html.

Trevor Project. "National Survey on LGBTQ Youth Mental Health 2020." Accessed February 12, 2021. https://www.thetrevorproject.org/survey-2020/.

CHAPTER 12:

Evon, Don. "Could Women Not Do These 9 Things in 1971?" *Snopes*, September 3, 2019. https://www.snopes.com/fact-check/9-things-women-could-not-do/.

Furman University. "Woman's Rights Petition to the New York Legislature, 1854." Accessed February, 19, 2021. http://history.furman.edu/~benson/docs/w-rights1.html.

Sawyer, Susan M. "The Age of Adolescence." The Lancet: Child and Adolescent Health 2, no. 3 (2018): 1.

CHAPTER 13:

Pulliam-Moore, Charles. "Women Significantly Outnumber Teenage Boys in Gamer Demographics." PBS, Aug 21, 2014. https://www.pbs.org/newshour/nation/female-adults-oust-teenage-boys-largest-gaming-demographic.

CHAPTER 14:

Emerson UU Marietta. "About Us: Our Vision and Mission." Accessed January 26, 2021. https://www.emersonuu.org/index.php/about-us/our-vision-and-mission/.

Harris, Sam. *Letter to a Christian Nation*. New York: Alfred A. Knopf, 2006.

CHAPTER 15:

Marie Forleo. "Glennon Doyle Talks Marriage, Sexuality & Choosing An Untamed Life." Mar 9, 2020. Video, 34:41. https://youtu.be/XhOxjFaga78.

CHAPTER 16:

American Psychological Association. "Psychology Topics: Depression." Accessed January 29, 2021. https://www.apa.org/topics/depression.

Armstrong, Thomas. "The Myth of the Normal Brain: Embracing Neurodiversity." AMA Journal of Ethics 17, no. 4 (2015): 348-352. https://doi.org/10.1001/journalofethics.2015.17.4.msoc1-1504.

Billings, Andrew, and Rudolph Moos. "Chronic and Non-Chronic Uni-Polar Depression: The Differential Role of Environmental Stressors and Resources." Journal of Nervous & Mental Diseases 172, no.2 (1984): 65–75. https://doi.org/10.1097/00005053-198402000-00001.

Institute for Quality and Efficiency in Health Care (IQWiG). "Depression: Experiences with Antidepressants." Last updated June 18, 2020. Accessed February 12, 2021. https://www.ncbi.nlm.nih.gov/books/NBK361002/.

CHAPTER 17:

Doyle, Glennon. Untamed. New York: Penguin Random House LLC, 2020.

Hattmaker, Jen. "Longing, Belonging and Faith." April 21, 2020. In Unlocking Us with Brene Brown. Produced by Brene Brown Education and Research Group, LLC. Podcast, MP3 audio, 82:13. https://brenebrown.com/podcast/brene-with-sue-monk-kidd-and-jen-hatmaker-on-longing-belonging-and-faith/.

Made in the USA
Columbia, SC
09 May 2021

37613295R00108